OVERVIEW

Overview

Sometimes work seems to combine unlimited needs with limited available resources. A situation like this sets up a world of immediate crises, rapidly shifting priorities, and reactive instead of proactive management. And these difficulties make it hard to focus on anything except the task right in front of you.

But managing work on a portfolio level takes projects, programs, and portfolios, and groups them together to facilitate their management. This ensures that they produce the planned benefits and meet the strategic business objectives that you're striving toward.

Managing from a portfolio perspective can give you both the high-level and wide-angle viewpoints needed to bring all the work under control.

Portfolio management, as set out by the Project Management Institute (PMI®), can reduce the chaos by enabling an organization to do the right work at the right time.

Portfolio management processes help to ensure the organization addresses the projects and programs that are the most essential to strategy execution and effective corporate performance.

While projects and programs are critical to organizational success, portfolio management extends beyond the simple completion of these components and focuses on strategic objectives and outcomes.

It changes how people work together – even across organizational boundaries – to accomplish project- based work.

Whether you are currently a portfolio manager or are just interested in the ideas involved in portfolio management, an increased understanding can give you a high-level perspective about how your work contributes to your company's goals.

This high-level view is what portfolio management is all about. Instead of viewing projects and programs in isolation, it allows you to consider the dependencies and interactions among these portfolio components, as well as between them and other organizational areas.

This book is aligned to PMI's® The Standard for Portfolio Management. The Standard for Portfolio Management expands on the work presented in A Guide to the Project Management Body of Knowledge (PMBOK® Guide) and the Organizational Project Management Maturity Model (OPM3®).

The Standard for Portfolio Management is PMI's® companion to the PMBOK® Guide. The Standard shows the links between portfolio management and program and project management, and between portfolio management and the organization.

Just as the PMBOK® Guide sets out the good practices for project management, The Standard for Portfolio Management presents a documented set of processes showing generally accepted good practices in the area of portfolio management.

In this book, you'll be introduced to the core concepts involved in portfolio management. You will discover how important it is to understand the management of portfolios, as well as learn about the relationships between portfolio management and project and program management.

You will also find out about the role of portfolio management within organizations, and about the roles and responsibilities of portfolio managers. You will be introduced to the links and relationships between portfolio management and organizational strategy, governance, and operations, and learn how metrics and reporting relate to it all.

"When in danger or in doubt, run in circles, scream and shout!" - Laurence J. Peters

This saying describes "life as we know it" in many organizations throughout the world.

According to AMR Research, as many as 75% of organizations surveyed in 2002 did not have a process for planning or monitoring which projects they approved, funded, and delivered.

Often, the squeaky executive gets the grease. That is, the most vocal and persistent executive obtains the funding for favored projects, which may or may not align with organizational strategies.

Life in such organizations is chaotic.

No one knows whether the approved projects will support organizational strategies and goals.

No one has a handle on how much the ongoing project work is costing the organization or whether existing resources will support all the development work going on.

And certainly no one will ever know whether projects actually pay for themselves and accrue the benefits their sponsors promise from them.

The project portfolio management processes put forth by the Project Management Institute (PMI®) are intended to reduce such chaos by injecting planning and monitoring processes into an organization's normal business cycle.

Portfolio management processes help to ensure that the organization addresses the projects and programs that are most essential to strategy execution and corporate performance.

In other words, portfolio management processes enable an organization to do the right work at the right time.

The Standard for Portfolio Management is PMI's guide to the project portfolio management (PPM) processes. The guide also focuses on portfolio management as it relates to the disciplines of program and project management.

The Standard for Portfolio Management is an expansion on "A Guide to the Project Management Body of Knowledge" (PMBOK® Guide) and "The Organizational Project Management Maturity Model" (OPM3®).

This book is designed to deepen your knowledge about the portfolio management processes and how they operate within the organization.

When you have completed this book, you will understand:

how the portfolio management processes function within the organization

You will learn about key stakeholder roles and responsibilities and what kinds of organizational influences affect portfolio management.

the importance of portfolio management processes and Process Groups

You will learn the characteristics of Process Groups and the processes performed by the two Portfolio Management Process Groups: the Aligning Process Group and the Monitoring and Controlling Process Group.

As you go through this book, you will be called upon to use your existing knowledge of project and program management. Portfolio management is simply project management "writ large."

For proper portfolio management, a moderate amount of knowledge and skill with project management practices and theories is required.

The first personal computer (PC), the Altair 8800, was released in 1975. It was a hobbyists' kit with limited functionality, but the revolution it kicked off would change the world forever.

Nobody could have predicted the explosion of PC sales, which went from a few thousand units in 1975 to annual sales in excess of 100 million personal computers by the year 2000. Nor could anyone have foreseen the many and varied uses to which PCs would be applied, or the thousands of pieces of hardware and software that sprung from the invention.

The high tech and computer industries changed incredibly fast. As the personal computer was an entirely new product, the potential sales were unknown and the possible uses for homes, businesses, and schools, as well as the eventual popularity of the Internet, were unexpected.

For you to have ended up as an owner of one of the giant PC companies, you would have needed effective, efficient, and integrated project and program management, and also constant monitoring and adjustment of the organization's strategic goals and objectives. In other words – portfolio management.

As the CEO of an emerging PC-manufacturing company, would you have needed portfolio management techniques when your market was a few thousand hobbyists? What about when you had to embrace and incorporate a strategic change as your customer base became 200,000 business and home users? How about when industry sales reached more than 100 million units per year?

Dominating the hobbyist market might not require portfolio management techniques, but dominating the worldwide market surely would. Although not all industries are as volatile – or have as constantly-shifting a landscape as the PC industry – the processes of portfolio management, which design portfolios to be efficient, effective, and aligned with your strategic goals, are vital to success in all kinds of organizations.

The PMBOK® Guide defines a portfolio as "A collection of projects or programs and other work that are grouped together to facilitate effective management of that work to meet strategic business objectives. The projects or programs of the portfolio may not necessarily be interdependent or directly related."

Portfolio management is the centralized management of one or more portfolios to achieve specific strategic business objectives.

Portfolio management includes processes for setting up portfolios in the best possible manner. Continued optimization is ensured by monitoring the performance and interaction of both the components and the portfolio as a whole.

Changes, even positive ones, may have effects on your business that require adjustments for optimum performance.

For example, greater-than-expected returns might result in overtaxed accounting departments. Fundamental strategy changes – such as your goals shifting from selling to hobbyists to marketing your product to home users, small businesses, governments, and major corporations – also require changes to the way you do business.

The portfolio management process is divided into two process groups:

the Aligning Process Group

Using criteria that ensures alignment with the organization's strategic plan, the Aligning Process Group determines how components will be categorized, evaluated, selected, and managed as part of the portfolio.

the Monitoring and Controlling Process Group

The Monitoring and Controlling Process Group reviews all data related to the portfolio and its components as to actual performance, continued alignment with strategic objectives, dependencies, and effective use of resources. It also takes a higher view, monitoring expected changes in the business environment, considering constraints that may affect performance, and ensuring that the portfolio itself performs as required by organizational rules.

The activities of the Aligning Process Group are based on the company's plan – an output of the Strategic Planning process. The Aligning Process Group's seven individual processes – Identification, Categorization, Evaluation, Selection, Prioritization, Portfolio Balancing, and Authorization – ensure all components tightly align to the strategic goals of the company. This process group also ensures the theoretical best mix of components and resources based on the information available.

But as projects and programs commence, real-world considerations – such as changes in scope, budget overruns, and missed deadlines – begin to affect component performance and therefore the performance of the portfolio as a whole.

The functions of the Monitoring and Controlling Process Group review and report on actual component and portfolio performance, and examine current and predicted business conditions for continued optimization. This process group's activities also incorporate any changes to the strategic plan, so the portfolio can adapt to changing conditions and goals.

This book examines the importance of the portfolio management processes and their interactions, and how to properly align, monitor, and control portfolios.

The basic activities, the tools and techniques, and the inputs and outputs associated with each of the processes are discussed. This book is aligned with the Project

Management Institute's® The Standard for Portfolio Management.

CHAPTER 1 - Introduction to Portfolio Management

CHAPTER 1 - Introduction to Portfolio Management

Section 1 - Portfolios and Portfolio Management

Section 1 - Portfolios and Portfolio Management

Portfolio management aligns all the components of a portfolio with strategic business objectives. As a result, it promotes the kind of success that just can't happen when multiple projects are managed individually.

Portfolio management provides a structure that allows portfolios, projects, and programs to be aligned with objectives. It allows the level of monitoring needed to ensure progress and process improvement, and it can improve overall operations by making the best possible use of resources.

In this lesson, you will learn to identify the common characteristics of portfolios and understand the differences in the management of projects, programs, and portfolios.

While portfolios can encompass a bewildering array of projects, programs, and other work, all these components have some common characteristics.

They all constitute investments made by the organization; they are all aligned with strategic business goals; they can be grouped to facilitate management; and they can all produce quantifiable metrics by which to measure success.

Portfolios need projects and programs in order to achieve strategies; they all share goals and resources. They all need to have regularly scheduled reviews in order to give pertinent information on portfolio components.

With so much in common – but with strategic differences as well – leadership, scope, planning and monitoring, and measurements of success need to be adjusted from project to program to portfolio.

The benefits of portfolio management

Bob is the program manager in charge of his small e-learning company's localization program. His tasks include managing specific courses being translated into other languages, as well as managing whole programs for each of the different language vendors.

Bob's projects and programs come in on time and on budget, but his Localization Department is still floundering. How can that be?

All the components of a portfolio – including individual projects and groups of projects called programs – have to align with what a company needs.

If not, the work can be done to perfection, beat scheduled deadlines, and even be under budget, and yet it still won't have the right impact on the bottom line.

So how does portfolio management relate to project management? For many years "project management" only referred to projects, which are defined by the PMBOK® Guide as temporary endeavors undertaken to create unique products, services, or results.

But in the past 20 years there has been a change, and today the concept includes program and portfolio management. While projects are temporary and have unique outputs, programs are groups of related projects that have coordinated management, and portfolios group together projects or programs as well as other work.

Management of both programs and portfolios gives benefits and a level of control that can't be achieved by individual project management. Program and portfolio management coordinate their components with the end goal of meeting strategic business objectives.

According to the **PMBOK®** Guide, portfolio management is the centralized management of one or more portfolios, which includes identifying, prioritizing, authorizing, managing, and controlling projects, programs, and other related work, to achieve specific strategic business objectives.

The benefits of understanding portfolio management are that it
- provides a framework for aligning portfolios, projects, and programs with organizational objectives,
- allows monitoring of projects and programs to ensure progress,
- can improve business operations through superior targeting of resources.

Perhaps some of your experiences could have been improved by a closer alignment of your project to strategic business goals. Portfolio management has the benefit of being able to provide a framework for alignment of portfolio components with organizational objectives.

A portfolio manager reviews all the potential projects and programs that might be included in the company's portfolio, and chooses only the ones that support strategic objectives. Portfolio managers also review current components, and if they don't support the organization's goals they are excluded before more resources are invested.

Portfolio management gives a structural framework for these reviews, and funding and support can be allocated based on strategic objectives such as risk categories, desired business lines, or infrastructure and internal process improvement.

Portfolio management also allows monitoring to ensure progress.

The projects or programs in a portfolio may not necessarily be interdependent or even be directly related to one another. But portfolio management can facilitate the monitoring that ensures best practices are followed on all of them, even when they have different goals or resources needed.

Following best practices in portfolio management means applying the skills, tools, and techniques that will improve the chances of success over an assortment of projects.

And lastly, using portfolio management tools and techniques can improve business operations through superior targeting of resources.

Portfolio management can maximize the value of the portfolio. Through careful project and program review, a manager can evaluate the portfolio's investments in projects and programs to ensure diversification, eliminate redundancies, and make the most efficient use of resources over more than one project.

Bob, the e-learning program manager, took the time to learn about portfolio management. He was impressed with how much it helped him realize why his best efforts weren't helping his company to the fullest extent possible.

Aligning with strategic goals

"Some of my programs had the ultimate goal of translating all of the courses in the course curriculum library. This wasn't aligned with the overall company strategic objective, which is to maximize return on investment (ROI).

Now I start off by translating only the best-selling courses, and go further in the library only when other courses are needed."

Monitoring for progress

"When civil unrest broke out in Russia, our translation project had to be put on hold in that country. I switched the graphic artists slated for the Russian project over to work on Polish courses.

This kind of high-level monitoring kept the Polish project moving very efficiently, and allowed me to keep trained workers available for when the Russian project came back online."

Improving operations

"Using a portfolio-level view, I was able to see that my company had been contracting quality assurance work to a different vendor for each language.

I eliminated redundancies when I realized that some of my resources were capable of handling more than one language – especially when the languages are related, such as with European French and Canadian French."

Question

Why is understanding portfolio management important?

Options:

1. It can improve business operations through superior targeting of resources

2. It provides a framework for aligning portfolios, projects, and programs with organizational objectives

3. It encourages various projects to be managed separately

4. It allows monitoring of projects and programs to ensure progress

5. It allows optimization of all resources, regardless of the financial outlay

Answer

Option 1: This is a correct option. Understanding portfolio management can eliminate redundancies and optimize the use of resources, resulting in improved business operations.

Option 2: This is a correct option. Portfolio management acts as a grid to allow portfolios, projects, and programs to be aligned with the strategic business goals of companies.

Option 3: This is an incorrect option. Portfolio management brings an understanding that projects and programs can be managed together at a high level, not separately.

Option 4: This is a correct option. Understanding portfolio management has the value of allowing the kind of evaluation that ensures projects and programs are progressing as they should.

Option 5: This is an incorrect option. Portfolio management does not disregard the financial costs of resources. Instead, it balances and diversifies the portfolio as a whole.

Characteristics of portfolios

When you hear the word "portfolio," what comes to mind? Perhaps you think of a financial portfolio, which is a group of varied securities held by investors.

Project portfolios do share similarities with financial portfolios, although there are obvious differences in inputs, tools and techniques, and outputs. Projects and programs – like financial investments – can be grouped for ease of management, and to quantify their associated risks and rewards.

And as with financial portfolio management, there is significant merit to wisely selecting and managing portfolio components.

According to the PMBOK® Guide, a project is a temporary undertaking with a specific outcome, while a program is a group of related projects. A project portfolio, then, is defined as a collection of projects or programs and other work that are grouped together to facilitate effective management of that work to meet strategic business objectives. The projects or programs of the portfolio may not necessarily be interdependent or directly related.

But portfolios are managed in a coordinated way, and that gives a level of control that can't be obtained from trying to manage each project or program individually.

There are four characteristics portfolio components share that allow them to have coordinated management. Understanding these characteristics of portfolios will help you follow best practices in portfolio management.

Their common characteristics are that they

constitute investments

Just as with financial portfolios, project portfolios are made up of resources – whether monetary outlay, infrastructure usage, or human resources – allocated among all the portfolio components.

Portfolio management helps establish a strategy for assessing proposed or current projects to create the right project investment mix for an organization.

are aligned with goals

Portfolios are managed by focusing on specific goals. For example, a fiscal goal might be to maximize the portfolio's value. If a project doesn't meet the company's strategic objectives, it shouldn't be included in the portfolio.

A diversification goal might include balancing the portfolio among various forms of project investments, or making the most efficient use of available resources.

can be grouped

Usually a portfolio is made up of a grouping of functions to be managed collectively. For example, a company might have an Accounting portfolio comprised of all of the work associated with functioning of the Accounting Department. This work would naturally be related.

Alternatively, a company might have a portfolio of its most important 25 projects, and the work associated with that portfolio's components is probably not related.

are quantifiable

There's a management saying that is just as true for portfolios as for projects; "You can't manage what you can't measure."

Using quantifiable metrics – such as ROI and risk estimates – portfolio managers can assess and manage projects, programs, and other related work.

Question

Portfolio managers can use metrics and alignment with goals to prioritize each component of a portfolio. But it's important to be able to identify the relationships between the components.

Match each component to its PMBOK® Guide definition.

Options:

A. Project

B. Program

C. Portfolio

Targets:

1. A temporary endeavor undertaken to create a unique product, service, or result

2. A collection of projects or programs and other work that are grouped together to facilitate effective management of that work to meet strategic business objectives

3. A group of related projects managed in a coordinated way to obtain benefits and control not available from managing them individually

Answer

This is the definition of a project. Projects are short-term, planned undertakings that can subdivide into sub-projects.

This is the definition of a portfolio. Portfolios encompass the flow of projects and programs from concept to completion.

This is the definition of a program. Programs are a layer above projects, and are defined in terms of constituent projects.

Portfolio management provides a holistic view of projects and programs across an enterprise, and ensures alignment with corporate strategy. As such, it includes discovering, approving, prioritizing, and generally managing portfolio components in order to achieve specific strategic business goals.

Ensuring alignment with strategy can be thought of as an organizational level of focus, which combines with the kind of project management level of focus that delivers projects effectively and efficiently.

The four common characteristics of portfolio components make it possible to achieve these two objectives simultaneously.

A consumer computer hardware manufacturer has four major product lines, including a line of laptops.

The company is working hard on a sub-line of ultra-lightweight laptops, which is under the management of Marie, the portfolio manager.

Marie has responsibility for the marketing and production of current products, and also for new product development.

Investments

The company invests $10 million in the production of the new laptop.

But Marie has to keep the other lines producing in addition to developing the ultra-lightweight, so the laptop investment is only part of the balanced portfolio budget.

Alignment with goals

The company is investing in the design and manufacture of the ultra-lightweight laptops in a focused attempt to reach a target of increased market share in the lighter laptop sales segment.

And just as there is a market-share goal for the ultra-lightweight laptop project, there are also goals for the whole laptop portfolio, including improving the value, efficiency, and quality of the whole product range.

Grouped together

Marie comes to the logical conclusion that the research, production, and marketing of all the laptop products should be grouped together in a portfolio, not just the individual projects for the ultra-lightweight.

Those projects – specific to the new product – form their own program.

Quantifiable metrics

The company CEO has stated his expectations for the product's return on investment (ROI) to be 5%, and Marie has measured the actual ROI as 5.25%, so there is a higher rate of return than expected. If there was an unfavorable ROI, Marie could make changes to decrease the difference.

She also has hard numbers about the cost and the resulting sales benefits of the subcomponents, such as the project for the online marketing of the new laptop. Decisions can be made about each component in the portfolio separately, based on how they help achieve the strategic objectives.

Marie has a big job on her hands. She is in charge of one of the four major product lines in her computer company, and there is a big push on to increase market share.

Being able to balance the company's investments in her portfolio and making sure all of the portfolio components align with strategic objectives are just good practices in portfolio management. In addition, grouping the components logically and quantifying results gives Marie the information she needs to properly manage all the work under her control.

Question

What are the characteristics that components of portfolios have in common?

Options:

1. They constitute investments made by the company
2. Unrelated components are managed individually
3. They are aligned with strategic goals
4. They have quantifiable metrics
5. They are investments made in the company
6. They can be grouped for management

Answer

Option 1: This is a correct option. Organizations invest in projects and programs, and portfolio management ensures that the investments are monitored and managed for efficiency and alignment with goals.

Option 2: This is an incorrect option. Although not all portfolio components are interdependent or related, they are grouped into a portfolio in order to be managed collectively.

Option 3: This is a correct option. A company sets specific strategic goals to improve the position of the company, and a portfolio manager makes project and program decisions based on these targets.

Option 4: This is a correct option. Portfolio components have specific measurable results. You can monitor them, compare them to goals and best practices, and make adjustments as necessary.

Option 5: This is an incorrect option. Portfolio components are internal investments made by the company, not external investments made by outsiders.

Option 6: This is a correct option. Instead of managing individual resources, portfolios group components to provide a high-level, holistic viewpoint.

Different management styles

"There are many ways of going forward, but only one way of standing still." – Franklin D. Roosevelt

In order to go forward into effective portfolio management, you have to avoid the trap of using only one management style.

Projects have beginnings and endings, and create one or more deliverables. Programs are umbrella organizations over a group of related projects, and are set up to deliver parts of a very large deliverable or set of deliverables. And portfolios encompass projects, programs, subportfolios, and other work, set up to align with strategic goals.

It just doesn't make sense to try and manage all these varied groupings of work in exactly the same way. Each category has specific attributes, and so needs its own management style to reach the highest possible peak of effectiveness.

The **PMBOK®** Guide defines portfolio management as the centralized management of one or more portfolios, which includes identifying, prioritizing, authorizing, managing, and controlling projects, programs, and other related work, to achieve specific strategic business objectives.

Effective portfolio management encompasses two different viewpoints: the high-level organizational focus that ensures all portfolio components meet the business's strategic objectives, and the task-level project-management focus that makes certain that deliverables are produced effectively and to expectations.

There are four general areas where clear differences can be distinguished in managing projects, programs, and portfolios:

- leadership,
- scope and change management,
- strategic planning and
- monitoring success measurement.

In your experience, you may have noticed a difference between projects, programs, and portfolios in leadership styles, and in who reports to whom.

A leader in management drives the business and ensures that value is received from the investments, no matter what they are. Projects, programs, and portfolios all need different leadership styles to be truly successful.

The three types of managers are

project managers

Project leaders are in charge of team members who do the work directly, such as technicians and specialists. As a result, project managers should be motivational team players with skills and knowledge about the task area. Project leadership is focused on product or service delivery that meets the directed criteria of success.

program managers

Programs need vision and leadership at a higher level to manage all the related projects and sub-projects. Program leaders manage project managers and smooth the progress of the politics of stakeholder management. So leadership for program managers focuses on relationships and conflict resolution.

portfolio managers

Portfolio leadership is leadership at a very high level, which includes portfolio management staff as direct reports. Portfolio management's focus is on adding value to portfolio decision-making, so portfolio managers need to supply vision and synthesis.

There are also differences in managing scope and change in projects, programs, and portfolios.

The scope of a project, program, or portfolio is the total amount of the work to be provided – the extent of the products, services, and results expected. The scope should include all the processes needed to complete the project successfully – and only those processes.

Scope creep or increase can occur concurrent with change, whether the change is from an additional customer request or as a result of the process itself.

Projects are specific to the products they deliver. So they have a narrow scope, and part of a project manager's task is to keep change to a minimum.

Programs include related projects, so their scope is wider. Program management includes an expectation of change, since the projects and scope most likely will have to change to meet the company's expectations. A program manager needs to embrace change.

Portfolios have a scope that is business-wide, and that transforms as the business's strategic goals change. Portfolio management includes continually monitoring changes in the general environment.

New Look Construction Company is a successful nationwide enterprise that has multiple projects going at all times. It has recently decided to ramp up its solar power capabilities, and has made that a strategic objective.

Three of its managers discuss their roles in leadership and scope management.

Chrissy

"My portfolio includes all of the East Coast construction projects, so I'm always balancing the need for expanding the company's interests in the solar market with the meat and potatoes commercial and home construction that makes up 75% of our business.

My portfolio staff and I have concerns that range from interdepartmental communication to legal liability, always making sure that we have the solar-power vision of the company in mind."

Andy

"I'm excited to be the program manager for the new solar power energy program. My projects include Research and Development, Production, Marketing, Technical Support, and Customer Service.

I work with a great team of project managers. At the moment, I'm about to present Chrissy with a request for additional research and development funds, because I'm happy to say that the scope of a project has been broadened."

Elaine

"My project is related to Andy's program – it's the production of a new low-cost solar laminate. I'm used to juggling my project resources – team members, budgets, equipment, and so forth – needed to meet my production numbers, but now my project has high visibility.

As a result, I have to tightly manage the change in scope. Andy and I just sat down and discussed the need for a new research and development engineer to join my team."

It's clear that differing styles of leadership, vision, and scope are needed for New Look Construction's managers.

Chrissy's focus is on the big picture and long-term benefits, balancing solar power's future market share against daily operating fiscal responsibilities.

Andy's focus is on the entire solar power program, and he doesn't worry about other construction projects or programs. And Elaine's whole concentration is on the laminate product her team is producing.

Question

Monty works for a retail chain that has both CD stores and consumer electronics discount outlets. He is responsible for the CD stores, where he communicates to individual store managers and to higher-level stakeholders.

He is in charge of general issues with stock and distribution and while he doesn't hire the individual clerks for each store, he does hire the managers.

Based on this information, is Monty a project, program, or portfolio manager?

Options:
1. Project
2. Program
3. Portfolio

Answer

Option 1: This is an incorrect option. The individual store managers could be considered to be project managers in this case, but Monty is concerned about more than one store.

Option 2: This is the correct option. Monty's direct reports are the individual stores' managers, and he manages all the stores in a related, collective way. This would indicate that he is a program manager.

Option 3: This is an incorrect option. Monty is in charge of all the CD stores, but not of the electronics stores. If he was in charge of both, he would likely be a portfolio manager.

Strategic planning includes defining and maturing the project scope, and identifying and scheduling the activities that need to happen for the project, program, or portfolio to succeed.

Monitoring is an essential part of getting feedback about the strategic plan, and involves collecting data about performance, producing metrics from that data, and reporting and communicating the performance information to stakeholders.

Project managers (PMs) plan in detail to manage the product deliverables. PMs monitor and control the tasks involved in the processes that create the product.

Program managers produce plans that give high-level guidance to projects, which then in turn give rise to detailed plans. It's both a top-down and a bottom-up approach. Organizational governance is the process by which an organization directs and controls its operational and strategic activities, and by which the organization responds to the legitimate rights, expectations, and desires of its stakeholders. In programs, governance structures are used to monitor projects and the ongoing work.

Portfolio managers plan the necessary processes and communication for the collective portfolio, and monitor the portfolio using aggregate performance and value indicators. So the communication plan and the processes used to manage the portfolio are directly affected by the aggregate components of the portfolio.

Successful measurement of work can happen in many ways. Managers need to use different techniques and metrics depending on the situation.

The three types of managers are

project managers

Success in managing projects is measured by the project's products being delivered on or under budget, on time, and to the stated specifications.

program managers

Program management success is measured through calculating return on investment (ROI), analyzing the program's new capabilities, and determining if the expected benefits of the program have been delivered.

portfolio managers

Successful portfolio management is determined by analyzing the aggregate performance of all the portfolio components.

At New Look Construction Company, Chrissy is the East Coast portfolio manager, Andy is the solar power program manager, and Elaine is the PM in charge of the solar laminate project. All three managers are in a status meeting.

Chrissy: So Elaine, your project is almost wrapped up, isn't it?

Elaine: Yes, it is, and I'm very pleased with how things went. After Andy and I determined that we needed an extra engineer, we got back on track. We ended up with a great product that actually exceeds the milliamps of current we were shooting for, and the project is on time and on budget.

Andy: That's right, and the laminate is a big boost to the whole solar power program. All the stakeholders are very pleased with the greater electrical output capacity, which will mean that the program as a whole will have no problems meeting the planned objectives.

Chrissy: You both have done a fantastic job. While our commercial construction numbers are not looking great, this project's success will mean we meet our overall targets.

Chrissy: If these numbers continue, when we reevaluate the portfolio we can adjust the program balance and increase the solar budget. The CEO will be happy, since we'll be keeping to our strategic objective of increasing our solar capabilities. Great work!

Different means of planning and monitoring, as well as measuring success, are needed for the different levels of work at New Look Construction Company.

Elaine, as PM, is focused on producing the solar laminate, and she monitors her resource needs accordingly. Her success is evident in the product, which came in on time, on budget, and with increased output.

Andy works with different PMs as he monitors and plans for the whole solar power program. He has an organizational governance strategy in place that allows him to operate and communicate in both directions – up to top management, and down to project management.

Chrissy, as portfolio manager, looks at the overall plan for her East Coast portfolio, of which the solar power program is only a part. She monitors on an aggregate component basis, and makes long-term decisions based on strategic objectives.

Question

Distinguish between project, program, and portfolio management. Some management types may have more than one example.

Options:

A. Project management

B. Program management

C. Portfolio management

Targets:

1. When management decided on a 20% cost reduction goal, Sue negotiated for a gradual reduction, then worked with all the PMs to achieve it

2. The new calcium supplement was manufactured within the time frame that Ruth expected

3. Megan makes sure that all the projects and other work align with the strategic goal of increasing the market share

4. Wendell considers all the relevant aspects of manufacturing the computer chip product

Answer

This is an example of program management. Leadership in programs requires negotiations both bottom-up and top-down.

This is an example of project management. Measuring a project's success is specific to how the product is produced and whether it gets delivered on time.

This is an example of portfolio management. Strategic planning and monitoring for portfolios needs high-level vision and adherence to goals.

This is an example of project management. A project's scope has a narrow focus on producing the product, and doesn't include information irrelevant to that.

There are, of course, many links between portfolio management and program and project management.

For instance, program and project information is used in portfolio reviews. Portfolio management and component management also work together to define termination criteria for components of a portfolio that are no longer effective, and they can work together in capacity planning.

Section 2 - Portfolio Management within the Organization

Section 2 - Portfolio Management within the Organization

Portfolio management has varied facets: it supports the corporation's vision and mission, allocates scarce financial resources efficiently and optimally, picks the right projects and fosters the right kind of innovation, and yields better priorities and faster times to market. And of course, the bottom line is to deliver winning results with positive financial impacts.

In this lesson, you will learn how portfolio management links with organizational strategy, governance, and operations; become familiar with the roles of a portfolio manager; and identify the metrics and reports used by portfolio management.

Management of ongoing operations and management of authorized programs and projects ensure that operations and portfolios are executed effectively and efficiently.

Governance processes provide the mechanisms that enable executives, managers, and professionals to integrate strategic planning with implementing and monitoring key activities.

Portfolio management helps organizations assign the right resources to the most important tasks based on the needs and strategic objectives of the business.

The end result is better alignment between portfolio investments and business decisions, as well as more efficient operations.

With knowledge of aligning and balancing, as well as monitoring and controlling, you can be sure you're on the best track to benefits realization.

And with skills in general leadership and management in addition to portfolio process improvement, you should feel confident enough to answer any help-wanted ad – even one for a portfolio management superhero.

Metrics and reporting are integral parts of all portfolio management. Metrics provide a quantitative way to analyze portfolio processes, and reporting uses metrics to aid in decision-making. Both are used to connect the goals of the organization to the project portfolio and keep all stakeholders involved in the portfolio's execution and results.

Portfolio management relationships

Bob is an e-Learning program manager in charge of his company's localization program. While Bob and his team perform well, the Localization Department as a whole is in bad shape.

The department has language projects going in too many skills areas and market segments. The company doesn't even sell to some of the markets, and there are pet projects that are way off strategy. There are also poorly performing projects that should have been killed long ago.

The department's portfolio is unfocused and has too many projects, resources are spread too thinly, and not all the components support the business strategy. Strategically, it's like a shotgun blast instead of a laser-sighted rifle.

No matter how well Bob performs his responsibilities, unless strategic alignment becomes a priority for the company the portfolio will never prosper. Bob's company needs to understand how portfolio management links with other activities.

Understanding the links gives two main benefits:

- knowing how project, program, and portfolio management work together to meet organizational goals,
- being able to see how effective portfolio management can maximize operational activities.

Project, program, and portfolio management work together to meet organizational goals. In fact, effectively defining a portfolio requires having a linked strategic objective. The portfolio is the expression of the strategy, so it and its components must support the organizational goals.

The portfolio links with business strategy through its project, program, and portfolio management functions. The competitive position of the business is maintained through supporting a strategy to increase sales and market share.

A portfolio achieves the organizational goal of balance – the right balance between long- and short-term work and high- and low-risk projects, all of which must be consistent with the business's goals.

It's also of value to be able to see how effective portfolio management can maximize operational activities. The strategic link with organizational goals focuses a portfolio by focusing its resources.

Such a focus avoids starting projects without enough resources. Portfolio management provides better objectivity in project selection, weeding out bad projects and ensuring the resources are available for the great projects. This gives a financial benefit since it maximizes return and productivity. And just as scarce resources are properly and efficiently allocated, efficient communication can also take place within the organization, both vertically and horizontally.

The portfolio management function outputs data that can be exchanged across the organization. Portfolio information is correlated with data from accounting, sales, and human resources. In turn, financial calculations and business decisions go back into the portfolio management process and from there to individual projects for implementation. All these links and levels of communication maximize operations.

A high-tech hardware manufacturer is facing some tough decisions. Which new products from the many opportunities available should get funding? And which ones will receive top priority and be accelerated to market?

Understanding how portfolio management links with other activities will help the company make the right decisions.

Meet goals

The manufacturing company develops criteria for project selection using the company mission of providing cutting-edge electronic components. This makes it easy to judge how well individual projects support the organization's objectives.

Today's new product projects can decide tomorrow's market profile, so knowing where you want your company to go is vital.

Maximize operational activities

The hardware manufacturing company uses goal-aligned management to make sure the right cutting-edge products get the resources and marketing needed to succeed.

Portfolio management and project prioritization are all about resource allocation. Using a strategic-goal focus will maximize return on investment, maximize research and development productivity, and ensure the company achieves its financial goals.

Question

Why is it important to understand how portfolio management links with other activities?

Options:

1. You can understand how project, program, and portfolio management work together to meet organizational goals

2. You can see how independent strategies balance a portfolio

3. You can see how effective portfolio management can maximize operational activities

4. You can learn how all resources can be supported, regardless of the financial outlay

Answer

Option 1: This is a correct option. Understanding how portfolio management links with other activities will let you see how all the components work together to achieve the underlying strategic objectives.

Option 2: This is an incorrect option. A portfolio and all its components are linked through an underlying strategic objective, so independent strategies are not used for each component.

Option 3: This is a correct option. Understanding the links between activities and portfolio management gives a greater understanding of how corporate-wide operations can be enhanced through resource allocation and goal-aligned decision-making.

Option 4: This is an incorrect option. Understanding the links between portfolio management and operational activities gives a greater ability to prioritize and allocate resources correctly – not just support all resources without regard to cost.

Links to organizational strategy

In building a house, you don't start digging the foundation without knowing how big the house will be. You start with a vision, which an architect turns into a plan in the form of blueprints. A general contractor uses that plan to manage each part of the building process, and reports back to you and to the architect.

It's the same way with portfolio management. Just as a foundation has to match the plan of a house's footprint, a portfolio needs to link with organizational strategy to fulfill its objectives.

Organizational strategy is formed from a company's vision and mission.

In business, the word vision refers to intentions or ideals that are broad and look to the future. It is the image that a business must have of its goals before it sets out to reach them. A vision statement is a short, succinct, and inspiring statement of what a company intends to become and to achieve. It describes hopes for the future, but it doesn't detail how the results will be accomplished.

A mission statement transforms a vision into a written form. It is a concrete documentation of the company's desired path and purpose. A mission statement should be brief, just laying out goals and priorities. The goals are particular objectives that relate to specific time periods and are stated in terms of facts.

The mission statement is concise, and has a customer perspective. It should answer three questions:

1. What does the company do?
2. How does the company do it?
3. For whom does the company do it?

Ben & Jerry's is dedicated to the creation and demonstration of a new corporate concept-linked prosperity.

To make, distribute, and sell the finest quality all-natural ice cream and euphoric concoctions with a continued commitment to incorporating wholesome, natural ingredients and promoting business practices that respect the Earth and the Environment.

Ben & Jerry's is dedicated to the creation and demonstration of a new corporate concept-linked prosperity.

We intend to become the single source of information technology for the home – Dell Computer Corporation. Dell's mission is to be the most successful computer company in the world at delivering the best customer experience in markets we serve. We intend to become the single source of information technology for the home – Dell Computer Corporation.

Once you have defined a vision and created a mission statement from it, you can begin to develop strategies that will move the organization toward that vision.

The triangle figure sets out the various organizational relationships. The top sections – the Vision, Mission, and Organizational Strategy and Objectives – show the targets or goals. The arrows in the triangle show how the element relationships are influenced by one another. These components steer all the actions that follow.

Question

Should the following statement from the telecommunications giant AT&T be classified as a company vision, or a mission?

"We are dedicated to being the world's best at bringing people together."

Options:

1. Vision
2. Mission

Answer

Option 1: This option is correct. This is a forward-thinking statement that encompasses a vision for the company, but does not lay out particular goals and priorities.

Option 2: This option is incorrect. A mission statement would take a desire and add concrete customer- focused targets.

Executive management creates a company vision and a mission. From those, organizational strategies and objectives are built.

The term "strategy" is broad, and describes looking at the bigger picture. Strategy is the way a company orients itself, both in its market and toward its competition. It is a plan to gain sustainable advantages. Successful companies have a strategic focus to their efforts, since a strategy adds value by consistently meeting customer needs better than the competition.

Organizational strategy and objectives are what set the goals for all portfolio management actions, allowing the correct allocation of resources and supporting the corporation's vision and mission.

A New York-based company with worldwide operations was struggling with its financial performance

after several project failures. Project investment decisions had historically been made on a case-by- case basis, rather than from a portfolio perspective.

Management now takes into account a 15-year planning horizon to realize growth, rather than just the traditional 3-year budget cycle. With this change, specific projects were stopped in favor of others that showed more promise. Also, project and program contributions have been clarified and communicated, and all leaders now have a clearer picture of what each is expected to deliver.

Planning and management are the processes that set up the actions needed to reach the goals. To implement the strategy, strategic management processes, systems, and tools are needed to define and develop high-level operations planning and management, and portfolio planning and management.

A US corporation operating in North America, Europe, and Asia had achieved considerable success based largely on its CEO's intuition-driven business decisions. This approach, however, became less effective as the company grew.

Now the CEO sets the vision and mission, but the specific management of the portfolios is what gets these targets realized.

Ivan is the IT portfolio manager for a large restaurant chain. Ivan's teams oversee all aspects of IT, from training and development to maintenance and support.

Ivan: Our organization has a new emphasis on service. Since the organizational strategy and objectives set the goals for what I have to do, I reviewed the portfolio to see if changes needed to be made in light of this new service emphasis.

Ivan: I found an imbalance when I discovered that the IT portfolio focused too strongly on new application development, and not enough on service and support.

Ivan: I used this information to set up the actions needed to reach our goal of better service. I decided to revamp all the help files and support web sites, and increase the training for the support personnel.

Ivan: These actions impacted everyone from restaurant managers to vendors, since everyone now has an easier time finding the information they need, and better support should any problems arise.

Organizations use the components of a portfolio – the projects and programs – to achieve strategic goals. Good portfolio management enables proper resource allocation, which is enhanced by managing to priorities.

The flow of control is as follows:

1. strategic intent and prioritization direct the allocation of the portfolio's overall financial resources,

2. the strategic intent maps onto the portfolio components and includes their individual resource allocations,

3. each program relates to a specific subset of the overall strategic intent, which it will deliver by using the resources allocated to it,

4. each project is defined by what it contributes to the portfolio's strategic intent, and is managed with this in mind.

Question

A pharmaceutical company has recently emerged in the marketplace, specializing in the field of psychiatric health. It derives its organizational objectives and translates them into a set of portfolios, including the implementation of a successful national marketing campaign. Its overall strategic intent is to be the leading provider of psychiatric products.

Identify examples of how portfolio management links with organizational strategy in this company.

Options:

1. The company's web site is updated to be more consumer oriented

2. An Internet marketing portfolio is created

3. A cost-cutting program is implemented

4. When the marketing director retires, the department is restructured to eliminate the position

Answer

Option 1: This is a correct option. This shows how the actions of project management are linked to the strategic goals through management of the marketing portfolio.

Option 2: This is a correct option, because the creation of this portfolio is a delegated subset of the overall strategic intent to be the leading provider of psychiatric products.

Option 3: This is an incorrect option. A cost-cutting program doesn't align with the strategic intent to be a leading provider of psychiatric products.

Option 4: This is an incorrect option. With a strategic intent that relies on marketing, eliminating this position will not help reach the goals.

Links to organizational governance

In the organizational relationships figure, the bottom of the triangle holds the management of operations and of projects. This level is where the operational activities are reviewed as to their ongoing creation of value, and program and project activities are compared in terms of new-value creation.

The discipline of portfolio management provides a consistent way to evaluate, select, prioritize, budget, and plan for the right projects – those that offer the greatest value to the company's strategic interests. But strategic planning is only part of the equation, since portfolios must also be governed.

The term "governance" describes the processes and systems an organization uses to function. Just as different countries have various systems of control or governments, corporate entities also have specific laws and customs under which they operate.

Governance as it pertains to portfolios refers to creating and using a framework to align and carry out portfolio management, since activities have to be undertaken in a clear, organized, and collective fashion if goals are to be met.

Governance includes issues of accountability and fiduciary duty, and governance processes use guidelines and controls to ensure good behavior, protect all stakeholders, and realize the anticipated value from portfolio investments.

Proper governance provides transparent pathways for different levels of involvement, decision-making, and the allocation and acceptance of responsibilities. These pathways are integral to the achievement of strategic goals and objectives.

Governance in an organization uses mechanisms of control such as phase gates, meetings, and progress-monitoring metrics. It oversees portfolio, program, and project management.

Executive management and operations management are interrelated, in that portfolio management is governed by executive management, and portfolio management governs project and program management.

Governed by

Portfolio management is governed by executive management. Organizational governance happens at various decision-making levels, and governance processes may differ in their focus and distribution of responsibilities.

But the processes always support specific goals and objectives, which are defined by executive management through the organization's strategic planning process.

Governs

Portfolio management governs project and program management and is the method by which strategic goals are achieved. Such governance is either through operations – the ongoing activities of the organization – or through the temporary work of projects.

Portfolio management defines how such activities are governed and is the link between programs or projects and executive management's strategic goals.

A large multinational banking group has a centralized information technology (IT) portfolio.

Two overlapping committees meet every three months to provide technology policy and oversight. The two groups meet right after each other, and sometimes hold joint sessions.

Governed by

One group is chaired by the senior vice president of the company. It brings together the senior marketing managers and includes the senior technology officer – the bank's top IT executive.

This overlapping structure gives the IT portfolio manager input and oversight from executives external to IT.

Governs

One of the groups is headed by the senior technology officer. It assembles all the IT portfolio project and program managers, but also includes the senior company vice president.

Including the senior vice president in the structure of IT portfolio management ensures that strategic goals and objectives are kept as integral components in decision-making.

Portfolio governance processes are created to ensure that value is received from the firm's portfolio investments. They need to be consistent with the overall governance of the firm.

One bank's governance processes might be different from another's in terms of focus and distribution of responsibilities. But the goal is to be consistent with each firm's strategic context and business intent, and effective in reaching business goals.

Question

How does portfolio management link to organizational governance?

Options:

1. Portfolio management is governed by program management

2. Portfolio management governs project and program management

3. Executive management is governed by portfolio management

4. Portfolio management is governed by executive management

Answer

Option 1: This is an incorrect option. Portfolios contain project and programs as components and have governance over them.

Option 2: This is a correct option. Portfolio management has control over its components and ensures their alignment with strategic goals.

Option 3: This is an incorrect option. While portfolio management might or might not be carried out by executives, it's executive management that has control over it.

Option 4: This is a correct option. Organizational relationships have a flow of control from executive management – at the top – down to portfolio management.

In smaller companies, the roles of executive and portfolio management might fall into the same area of responsibility. No matter what the size, however, governance gives an organization a consistent, accountable body for decision-making.

Links between operations and portfolios

You might think that surgical operations and business operations have nothing in common. But just as surgery produces value from a hospital's assets by means of a healthy patient and increased hospital income, business operations harvest value from the assets owned by organizations.

And as with surgical operations, organizational operations need high-level planning, precision in execution, and monitoring.

The **PMBOK®** Guide defines "operations" as "An organizational function performing the ongoing execution of activities that produce the same product or provide a repetitive service." In other words, it's a term used for the everyday activities of an organization. But the day-to-day procedures of a company are also related to portfolio management.

Imagine a company trying to make a few changes in its day-to-day operations. If the people responsible for implementing changes lack the authority and cross-functional span-of-control needed, no improvement will happen. And if changes do manage to take place, there still needs to be a portfolio-

management viewpoint. Otherwise, the changes might help one area at the expense of another, and do more harm than good.

Portfolio management is vital in this case, since it addresses itself to the gaps that exist between projects and the operational functions of the enterprise. Portfolios are the hub, ensuring that the selected projects align with the business strategies and produce the maximum benefits possible from the organization's limited resources.

There are two important links between portfolio management and operations:

- portfolio management produces outputs used by operations,
- operational activities influence a portfolio's success.

Portfolio management produces outputs that operations use.

Since operations involve overall organizational processes – such as production operations, manufacturing operations, and accounting operations – the activities are not always specific to a certain project. But the processes that operational management uses are often the end results of portfolio components being executed.

Portfolio management helps to align day-to-day operational requirements with the available resources. In this way it delivers project and program management solutions, answering the key question of "With the resources I have, how can I carry out my day-to-day plans?"

Portfolio management is also concerned with the planning of both proposed and active projects. Through portfolio component selection, better project portfolios are developed – which gives more opportunities for increased benefits. Portfolio management supports rational operational analysis and decision-making.

Portfolio management serves as a database for portfolio – and thus, operational – data, and as a link to other associated data. It also is a communication and monitoring system for information regarding projects, programs, and process changes.

A computer hardware manufacturing company has a training division within the Human Resources Department. Each type of training is a separate portfolio. The IT training portfolio manager, Helen, manages a number of current courses on an ongoing basis, but she is constantly being called upon to develop new technical courses to support the IT function. Helen's management of the portfolio produces outputs that are then used by operations.

Communications

"I spend a lot of time talking to and e-mailing the management stakeholders and the course development teams. My communication process is consistent so no one is overlooked and everyone has a common vocabulary and clear definition of responsibilities.

I find that ongoing communication helps maintain stakeholders' confidence and support. In addition, communication among the teams responsible for the various components ensures coordination and effectiveness of operations."

Resource management

"When we're planning for a new series of technical courses, it helps to have a portfolio-level overview of skilled resource availability. Looking at the whole portfolio of components means that I can identify what skills and qualifications are needed for operational success.

Then as the course developers finish one course, they go back into the general HR pool. So daily operations managers can choose developers according to availability and specialty."

Portfolio events or milestones need to be communicated both inside and outside the organization. This could include achievement of a major objective, elimination of a component, and other matters requiring corporate communications. Operational failures can often be traced to a lack of shared understanding of terminology, processes, and goals.

Portfolio management also needs to address any organizational impacts of changes, particularly in terms of resource management.

Question

Is the following statement true, or false?

"Portfolio management has an influence on project operations."

Options:

1. True
2. False

Answer

Option 1: The statement is true. Portfolio management produces outputs that are used in daily operations. The reverse is also true, however; operational functions also have an impact on portfolio management.

Option 2: The statement is not false. Portfolio management does influence daily operations. It is also true, though, that operations impact portfolio management.

The other side of the story is that operational activities influence a portfolio's success.

Portfolio component deliverables often generate ongoing work needed to fully realize planned benefits. Effective management of this work is critical to realizing the portfolio's expected value. And operational metrics certainly affect portfolio decisions – particularly regarding resource allocation.

So the portfolio management process has to take operational issues, processes, and results into account through the whole management cycle.

A consumer hardware manufacturer has four major computer product lines. The line of laptops has a sub-line of ultra-lightweight laptops under the management of Marie, the portfolio manager.

Marie is responsible for the marketing and production of current products, as well as new product development. She finds that operational activities influence her portfolio's success.

Financial success

"With my company's investment of $10 million in the production of the new laptops, of course I have to consider financial goals and objectives.

So in my management of the portfolio, I monitor component budgets, compare project spending with the allocated budgets, and analyze what benefits have been realized. Efficiency in operations reduces costs from R&D, labor, and many other areas."

Marketing success

"The company is investing in the ultra-lightweight laptops to increase our market share in the lighter laptop sales segment. Input from the operations of the marketing function is vital to our success.

For instance, we use this input to make strategic decisions about what criteria we use to choose and manage portfolio components. It will also let us see if our market share really does increase."

When the results of project status and performance are fed back into the portfolio management system, a loop is created that ensures that strategic goals are always taken into account. All of the portfolio management and operational processes are connected, even when a direct link isn't seen.

After all, key operational information collected about the portfolio components is critical in determining both the cost and value of an asset to the business.

Question

Identify the examples of how day-to-day operations interact with portfolio management.

Options:

1. Component processes are monitored using relevant metrics, and go/kill decisions made

2. A programmer is diverted from development to an urgent production task

3. Redundancy of duplicate manufacturing processes was eliminated, increasing the profit margin

4. A help-desk incident is recorded by the Level 2 team

5. The hybrid generator project was a stand-alone pet project of the senior VP, who monitored it

Answer

Option 1: This is a correct option. This is an example of portfolio management and operational activities linking to increase overall portfolio success.

Option 2: This is a correct option. This is an example of portfolio management producing outputs that are used by operations, since it is critical to know the relative importance of the different tasks before making resource changes.

Option 3: This is a correct option. This is an example of increasing the efficiency of operational activities, leading to an increase in a portfolio's success.

Option 4: This is an incorrect option. While this is an example of an operational activity, the link between it and portfolio management is not shown.

Option 5: This is an incorrect option. Independent projects like this usually don't align with strategic goals and aren't part of a portfolio.

Benefits realization

WANTED:

Portfolio manager with superhuman powers. Must be able to capture true cost/benefit comparisons of portfolio components, convey bad news through the minefields of executive hypersensitivity, and have superpowers of prioritization. Must be able to use the mind to manipulate and control components to transform hypothetical projects into a stream of actualized benefits.

You don't need to be a comic-book hero to be able to excel in portfolio management, but you do need to have a thorough understanding of the roles and responsibilities needed.

Portfolio management integrates various methods and techniques to change management's primary focus from the old ideal of "doing the work right" to the modern vision of "doing the right work." A portfolio manager has many roles to play, and needs diverse skills in order to do so effectively.

The portfolio manager leads the development of the company's portfolio; manages the portfolio; reports to key stakeholders; performs financial and what-if analyses to evaluate processes to improve project flow and delivery times; and often facilitates governance.

Most of the key processes in portfolio management support the ranking of potential projects based on value, benefits, risk, and alignment with organizational strategies – with the focus always on maximizing the realization of benefits.

Through the selection and execution of projects and programs in the portfolio, portfolio managers help ensure that firms continue to thrive in a world of constant change and competition.

The key roles they play in positioning organizations for increased strength and profitability are in

realizing the benefits

Benefits get realized by making sure there is an optimum balance of components and alignment with strategic goals.

To realize all the benefits from portfolio components, managers must align and balance the portfolio, then monitor and control the portfolio.

managing effectively

Effective portfolio management needs a high level of general management skills, such as decision-making and team-building skills.

But it also requires an ability to improve the management process itself, changing the prioritization criteria or metrics when needed.

Question

Identify the roles and responsibilities of portfolio managers.

Options:

1. Align and balance the portfolio
2. Operations management
3. General management and leadership
4. Monitor and control the portfolio
5. Set the corporate mission
6. Portfolio process improvement

Answer

Option 1: This option is correct. Aligning and balancing the portfolio with the strategic objectives is important in realizing all the planned benefits.

Option 2: This is an incorrect option. Portfolio management is linked to operations management, but portfolio managers do not control day-to-day corporate operations.

Option 3: This option is correct. Managing effectively requires both general management skills and portfolio-specific management skills.

Option 4: This option is correct. To realize the benefits from portfolio components, the portfolio must be monitored and adjusted or controlled as needed.

Option 5: This is an incorrect option. Mission-setting is done by the founder or top executive, and is not the responsibility of portfolio managers.

Option 6: This option is correct. Effective management requires a solid understanding of the portfolio process in order to enable continuous improvement.

Portfolio managers are key to benefits realization. The skills needed to accomplish this are both fiscal and nonfiscal, since strategic goals encompass more than raw profit.

Realizing benefits requires two process skill sets: the ability to align and balance the portfolio; and the ability to monitor and control the portfolio.

Throughout the entire portfolio management process, many decisions are made concerning the overall contribution of the components to the organization.

To optimize benefits realization, a portfolio manager has to understand the organization's vision, mission, and strategy and align and balance the portfolio in accordance with it. To accomplish this, managers

- identify, categorize, and evaluate all current and proposed projects relative to the organization's strategic direction,
- select and prioritize components based on their benefit to the organization,
- balance the portfolio's funding, resources, and risk, and authorize the work to begin.

These many decisions are the basis for portfolio components being selected, prioritized, and approved based on how well they align with organizational goals. Portfolio management also establishes criteria for terminating projects before completion, if necessary.

The decisions also balance the portfolio to determine a viable project mix – one that is capable of meeting the goals of the organization.

The other roles in portfolio benefits realization are

monitoring

A portfolio manager needs analytical skills to monitor the portfolio using performance reports and metrics, and be able to report actual benefits relative to intended benefits over the long term.

Monitoring and reporting include full-cycle governance of projects, programs, and portfolios. Encompassing a view from initial concept to final payment – rather than just from design to delivery – gives accountability and effective measurement.

controlling

Controlling the portfolio means being able to make adjustments as needed. If corporate strategy changes, a corresponding review of portfolio components should take place.

Strategic change often signals the need to add, modify, or remove some components so the portfolio remains aligned.

New Look Construction is a large nationwide organization that has decided to ramp up its solar capabilities. Since solar power construction is now a strategic objective, Chrissy – the East Coast portfolio manager – reviews her projects and programs.

Align

Chrissy examines the list of candidate projects for the coming year and approves three new projects that align with the solar strategy, including a project to design a commercial solar collector.

Balance

For inclusion in her portfolio, Chrissy selects projects and programs based on the risks and rewards of each one. This enables the management team to monitor the components closely and move resources among them appropriately.

Monitor

Chrissy gathers and reports on performance indicators and reviews the portfolio at scheduled intervals to ensure alignment is maintained with the solar ramp-up strategy.

Control

An older solar concentrator project is found to be no longer valid in light of new solar-laminate technology, so Chrissy eliminates it from the portfolio.

Question

Identify the roles and responsibilities of portfolio managers as they pertain to the realization of benefits.

Options:

1. Select and prioritize components based on the organization's goals, and review the portfolio for risk/return balance

2. Measure planned-to-actual performance and re-examine the portfolio while ensuring the component work is done effectively and efficiently

3. Determine a new chain of command and organization chart for the company

4. Oversee the production of individual products

Answer

Option 1: This option is correct. These are the responsibilities of portfolio management that will result in the alignment and balancing of the portfolio.

Option 2: This option is correct. Monitoring and controlling the portfolio is accomplished through measurement and adjustment of the components.

Option 3: This is an incorrect option. While a portfolio manager may have input into chain-of-command decisions, such changes don't pertain to benefits realization.

Option 4: This is an incorrect option. Production of temporary endeavors such as individual products is the responsibility of a project manager, not a portfolio manager.

Effective portfolio management

The other important area of responsibility for portfolio managers is to be able to manage effectively. In order to accomplish this, they must have a mix of various skills in the areas of

general management

General management skills include decision-making skills, knowledge of program and project management techniques, and general leadership and managerial skills.

Reporting is an essential part of portfolio management, so excellent communication skills are also needed.

process improvement

Strong process development skills are needed to develop the most suitable portfolio management process.

Knowledge of the techniques used for continuous improvement is also critical. With this knowledge, you can determine whether current management approaches are lacking or failing, and how to make the needed adjustments.

The roles and responsibilities of a portfolio manager in terms of general management are

- to be a strong facilitator, with the ability to drive a group to a decision,
- to consult and interact with all levels of management using tact and diplomacy,
- to interpret basic financial analysis and budget information,
- to collect, analyze, and clearly present data,
- to have general business acumen as well as industry-specific knowledge,
- to create and maintain relationships across the organization,
- to be able to estimate resource capacity against resource demand.

Reporting responsibilities include providing all stakeholders with performance assessments that are timely and accurate.

Early identification and notification of portfolio-level issues and risks is vital, so any areas that are impacting performance can have the proper intervention.

Performance assessments collect, organize, and circulate information on how the portfolio resources are being used to complete the strategic objectives.

Performance reporting involves the following:

1. status reports – how the project or program is right now,

2. progress reports – how complete the work is now, and how much more work remains,

3. forecasting – determining if the project or program will end on schedule and on budget, and estimating how much longer the work will take, and how much more money it will need,

4. scope – how the project is meeting the project scope,

5. quality – what the results of quality audit, testing, and analysis are,

6. risks – what risks have entered and what their effect has been on the project or program.

General management skills aren't the only ones needed, however. Process improvement skills are vital for continuous improvement and tight alignment with strategic objectives. Performance reports help immeasurably in process improvement.

Improving portfolio management processes includes managing the development and definition of the prioritization model. In this way you can shift from a free-for-all competition for resources to a disciplined objectives-oriented approach.

At New Look Construction Company, Chrissy is the East Coast portfolio manager. She is talking to Andy, the solar power program manager.

Chrissy: When our new strategic focus on solar power was first implemented, there was a lot of confusion, remember?

Andy: There sure was. It seemed like everyone was worried about what would happen. I was in a whole other department, and didn't know if I'd still have a job.

Chrissy: I made sure I got all the facts and then spent a lot of time in meetings with you guys – with all the project and program managers, in fact.

Chrissy: Being proactive in communicating the changes went a long way to dispel rumors and concern. It also kept production high even during a time of change.

Andy: It was good leadership. The change in the objective, though, meant that you had to decide if projects or programs needed to be terminated early. That couldn't have been easy.

Chrissy: Well, that's true. But it also gave me a great opportunity to re- evaluate our whole process and bring everything back into tight alignment with the new goals.

New Look Construction is lucky to have a portfolio manager like Chrissy. She has the general skills of leadership, decision-making, and communication, and her direct reports appreciate her.

She also embraces change instead of running from it, and uses change as a springboard for process improvement.

Question

Identify the roles and responsibilities needed for effective management of portfolios.

Options:

1. Lead, manage change and budgets, and communicate effectively

2. Develop, define, and re-evaluate prioritization models and governance criteria

3. Manage individual projects with a keen eye for detail

4. Ensure that customer support is the highest priority

Answer

Option 1: This option is correct. These are all examples of the types of general management skills needed to be effective.

Option 2: This option is correct. Developing and changing the portfolio process when needed is an example of process improvement skills.

Option 3: This option is incorrect. It's good for a portfolio manager to know general project management skills, but the actual project management should be done by the PM.

Option 4: This option is incorrect. Some companies may adopt customer support as their highest priority, but it is an example of a mission, not a portfolio management role.

When analyzing the effectiveness of a portfolio manager, it's important to look at two main areas: the ability to use the processes that achieve the realization of planned benefits, and the possession of management skills in both general and portfolio-specific areas.

Joe was able to align, monitor, and control the portfolio management process, as well as find ways to improve it. He played an important role in supporting the overall strategy of the organization and demonstrated general management skills in preparing and disseminating information to all the parties involved.

In the final analysis, it's clear that Joe knows the roles and responsibilities of the portfolio manager, and executes them well.

Case Study: Question 1 of 2
Scenario

Betsy is a portfolio manager for a multi-state health group that provides care in nine different regions in the US. The group has medical centers in five states and outpatient facilities throughout the care region.

The strategic objective for her company is to increase the level of quality of the health care provided. Answer the questions to determine Betsy's effectiveness as a portfolio manager.

Question

After weighing the proposed cost and double-checking her budget, Betsy decides to add a program that will upgrade all the firm's older radiology equipment. She starts with MRI machines because the CEO requested it, and delegates the program management to her new intern.

In what ways is Betsy being an effective portfolio manager?

Options:

1. Adding the radiology upgrade program
2. Checking costs and funding
3. Delegating to her intern
4. Deciding to upgrade the MRI machines first

Answer

Option 1: This is a correct option. Adding this program will align Betsy's portfolio well with the strategic initiative. It is effective portfolio management that will lead to the realization of benefits in the area of quality.

Option 2: This is a correct option. This is an example of effective portfolio management because Betsy's ability to interpret financial analysis and budget information will help her company realize fiscal benefits.

Option 3: This is an incorrect option. Using an inexperienced intern as a program manager is not making the best use of resources and is a poor management choice.

Option 4: This is an incorrect option. Using a pet project – even a CEO's pet project – as the basis for portfolio decisions won't help achieve benefits realization.

Case Study: Question 2 of 2

Betsy receives updates on the schedule of the new nursing home project and is concerned about its delays impacting the organization's cash flow. She sends reports to all the financial stakeholders of the nursing home project. She also proactively began figuring out why the delays were happening.

In what ways is she demonstrating effective portfolio management?

Options:

1. Aligning the goal to the process
2. Getting updated about the nursing home delay
3. Reporting on the nursing home project
4. Troubleshooting proactively

Answer

Option 1: This is an incorrect option. Betsy didn't align the goal to the process, nor should she. In this situation, she should try and determine whether her current management approaches are effective.

Option 2: This is a correct option. Making sure she has full access to communications is effective portfolio management, particularly when one of her projects is experiencing challenges.

Option 3: This is an incorrect option. While performance reporting is good portfolio management, all the stakeholders need to be informed, not just financial stakeholders.

Option 4: This is a correct option. Finding the reasons behind problems is an excellent general management skill that will lead to process improvements.

In the area of benefits realization, Betsy does a good job aligning the portfolio to the strategic quality objective by adding the equipment upgrade program to her portfolio. But she doesn't make the best choices when she uses a pet project as rationale for determining where to begin, or when she delegates to an inexperienced intern.

She has some effective management skills and works to improve the portfolio management process when she troubleshoots the nursing home delays. She does not, however, understand the portfolio reporting process well enough to include all the relevant stakeholders in her communications.

In other words, Betsy successfully executes some of the roles and responsibilities of the portfolio manager, but would benefit from more knowledge.

Portfolio management metrics

NPV, ROI, EV, KPI, PCT...sometimes learning about portfolio management can make you feel as though you're drowning in a sea of alphabet soup.

All the initials just listed stand for various organizational metrics. Metrics are the measurements used to improve portfolio processes by determining if the portfolio is meeting its objectives. From finances to milestones, everything needs to be measured and reported on.

Understanding portfolio metrics and reporting processes will enable you to make sense of the sea of acronyms.

Metrics are standards of measurement used for quantitative assessments. They determine numerical, exact amounts or proportions of something.

Sorin Dumitrascu

These measurements can address the process that needs to be quantified, the procedures to carry out the measurement, and the procedures to interpret the data as compared to previous or similar assessments.

They can be used to track resources, productivity, trends, financial returns, and much more.

Portfolio management uses metrics to examine three functional areas: fit, utility, and balance. The first area, fit, looks at the projects currently being worked on. There need to be solid reasons for selecting and prioritizing the projects, so criteria that take the strategic objectives into account have to be developed. In addition to reviewing current projects, these criteria are applied to new components being considered for funding.

The next area is utility. This is where the value of the project or program is defined by costs, benefits, and associated risks. The most critical projects and programs are measured against predetermined metrics that relate right back to the strategic objectives. These yield quantifiable data, ensuring that the planned costs, benefits, and risks are accurate.

The final area is balance. Here, information is validated and decisions made. To align with strategic goals, the total portfolio must be optimized, not just a single project. Without metrics, it's impossible to determine the fit, utility, or balance of a portfolio.

Typically, the metrics tracked in portfolio management are key performance indicators (KPIs).

As explained in the PMBOK® Guide, "A Key Performance Indicator can be a direct measurement or an expert assessment. When a Key Performance Indicator is quantitative, involving direct measurement, a form of metric is required. A metric is a measurement of something. Something tangible, such as an error count, can be measured directly and objectively. Something intangible, such as customer satisfaction, must first be made tangible – for example, through a survey resulting in ratings on a scale – before it can be measured."

Metrics are used to show the value of the portfolio to the organization. Metrics can take several overall forms:

binary

If a metric is measuring a simple state of whether or not something exists, it is an either/or proposition – which is known as a binary metric. A determination of quality using a pass-or-fail rating is an example from the manufacturing industry.

complex

When measuring along a rating scale, metrics may be quite complex. Scales may be numerical – such as temperature scales – or measured in conjunction with other scales – such as pressure. Or they may rate inherently qualitative characteristics – such as customer satisfaction – so quantitative calculations may be done.

monetary

Metrics may even be economic or monetary, such as measuring the financial return received on an investment.

Question

A hospital conducted an employee opinion survey. One of the questions asked was, "Are you in favor of the new overtime policy?"

What form of metric does this question fall into?

Options:

1. Binary
2. Complex

3. Financial
Answer
Option 1: This option is correct. This question can only have a yes-or-no response, which makes it a binary form of metric.

Option 2: This option is incorrect. The question as phrased can only have a simple yes-or-no answer, so it is not a complex form of metric.

Option 3: This option is incorrect. The question does not ask for nor generate any monetary information, so it is not a financial metric.

Two of the most important categories of metrics needed in portfolio management are financial measures

milestone measures

Financial measurements include all types of data related to monetary investment in the portfolio and in its components. Financial metrics include return on investment (ROI), net present value (NPV), and the distribution of the funding with regard to the strategic goals.

Financial metrics can include those overhead expenses directly related to a portfolio, such as administrative expenses, salaries, legal expenses, and so on.

Milestone measurements measure how closely the achievement of goals or landmarks matches to what was planned. Statistics such as budgeted vs. actual costs, customer satisfaction scores, percent of scheduled work complete, and product delivery performance are common.

There are a variety of other measurements more specific to particular organizations or industries, such as measuring commitments as opposed to closed contracts in sales. Or work allocation balancing may be useful, since it tracks targets for types of work. For instance, if a car dealership wants at least 45% of its portfolio workload to come from repair work, it can track the actual repair work percentage.

Laurie is a portfolio manager at a leading boot factory. She uses both categories of metrics to help her describe her portfolio's progress toward the targets her company has established.

Milestone

"We have very high quality targets, so we collect quality milestone data from both our operations and customer support teams. We look at the internal defect rates as DPMO, or defects per million opportunities.

We get our customers' responses to surveys in which they rate their satisfaction with the quality of their boot purchases. For their ease of use, the scale is rated as poor, acceptable, and high. We then translate these responses into hard numerical data."

Financial

"We collect financial data on per-person downtime. This metric tells us the financial cost of the hours employees spend between assignments.

Downtime can happen if a person comes off a project and doesn't immediately have another job assignment, and we like to see this number as low as possible, and always trending downward."

Question

Match each metric category to examples. Not all the examples will have a match.

Options:

A. Financial

B. Milestone
Targets:
1. NPV, or net present value of all expected cash flows
2. ROI, or return on investment
3. PCT, or percent of scheduled work complete
4. Failure analysis begun
Answer
This is an example of a financial metric. NPV is the difference between the present value of the cash inflows and the present value of the cash outflows, making it financial data.

This is an example of a financial metric, since it is information about the monetary return on an investment.

This is an example of a milestone category of metric. Milestone metrics describe progress toward goals, which includes determining how close you are to completion.

This is not an example of a metric, and should not be selected. Failure analysis looks for causes and is not defined numerically.

Portfolio management reporting

Any strategic initiative is accompanied by a vast amount of information. But all those inputs and outputs have to be evaluated, sorted, structured, and retained in order to make maximum use of the information.

Portfolio management generates quantities of metrics that can affect not only daily operations of the organization, but the company's future direction as well.

For instance, calculating ROI in different areas can show which projects or programs contribute the most, allowing priorities to be established for the highest impact. Programs that are inefficient or not making the best progress toward the strategic objectives can be redesigned or discontinued.

It seems like everything is in the public view today. Prompted by events such as scandals and industry bailouts, the end result is that the business world has seen

Sorin Dumitrascu

a positive trend toward greater corporate accountability and transparent governance.

And accountability includes not only documenting negative situations that need improvement, but showing the value that has been captured by the various areas of the organization.

For portfolio management, this means being able to use quantifiable measurements to show how the various portfolio components and the portfolio as a whole contribute to the organization. It brings a focus on results that improves the effectiveness of the process as a whole.

It also ensures there is effective communication between the project managers, portfolio managers, portfolio sponsors, and portfolio stakeholders.

Portfolio reporting involves obtaining relevant information about the portfolio's progress and conveying it to interested parties. Such reporting is tightly linked to other areas of the organization that have an influence on portfolio priorities, balancing, and overall direction.

There are sophisticated portfolio management and financial software systems available to help track actual performance against cost and schedule criteria. These same systems can aid in the reporting of the data and analytical evaluation.

There are several feasible forms of measurement to analyze portfolio performance and content. The two general categories are program-and-project reporting, and financial reporting.

For both categories, preliminary setup should include
- identification of the key portfolio reports needed for your organization, which may include

financial, resource utilization, benefits realization, or risk reports,

- establishment of a tailored project portfolio communications platform, with e-mail notifications at workflow gates.

When setting up your portfolio reporting, you need to decide on a framework. While it is vital to ensure you are receiving timely project status reports for all projects and programs in the portfolio, the information should also

- be modeled in a spreadsheet or in project software,
- be presented in ranked order, sorting the columns as needed,
- indicate in which fiscal year a strategic initiative will be completed, and whether the initiative is active,
- pending, closed, or canceled,
- be gathered on a set schedule for producing and updating the portfolio reports – often this is done weekly or monthly.

Question

What do the general categories of portfolio reporting include?

Options:

1. Status and analysis of project, program, and portfolio performance
2. Human resources status
3. Financial status and analysis
4. Status and analysis of project performance only

Answer

Option 1: This option is correct. One of the major categories of portfolio reporting is analyzing the status of portfolio components and of the portfolio as a whole.

Option 2: This option is incorrect. While HR status may be included as part of the portfolio status reporting, it is not a general category of reporting by itself.

Option 3: This option is correct. One of the major categories of portfolio reporting is analyzing financial data and determining the portfolio's financial status.

Option 4: This option is incorrect. Portfolio reporting responsibilities encompass all portfolio components, not just projects.

Reports can be configured to track status across projects, programs, or portfolios. The four major categories of program-and-project reporting are

enterprise strategic goal achievement

Goal achievement reports show to what degree portfolio components factor into the realization of the organization's strategic goals.

enterprise asset maintenance and development

Asset reports demonstrate how portfolio components contribute to the maintenance and development of particular assets in the organization.

enterprise risk profile

Risk profile reports detail the component risks for the organization.

enterprise resource capability

Resource capability reports show each component's planned and actual resource usage.

Mike is a portfolio manager for an auto parts manufacturer.

In his portfolio management process, he uses metrics for the four major categories of program-and- project reporting.

Enterprise strategic goal achievement

The company has had problems with customers rejecting their delivered orders due to excessive parts substitutions. The new goal is to minimize rework of customer work orders. The metrics used are the KPIs of work orders complete with no more than 10% substitution, and the percentage of internal, proactive work orders, which fix potential problems up front.

Mike tracks the status toward the strategic goal by reporting on completion compliance and assessing the number of internal work orders generated.

Enterprise asset maintenance and development

Mike has a goal to maximize the plant's uptime. He uses metrics on the number of emergency work orders on critical systems, inspection compliance, and protective device maintenance compliance.

These enable him to analyze and preserve the plant's asset maintenance and integrity.

Enterprise risk profile

To analyze the portfolio component risk for the organization, Mike uses metrics such as a safety performance index, the number of significant workplace accidents, and total days lost due to injury.

He can then determine the risk status and profile by reporting on the safety-audited operational capabilities.

Enterprise resource capability

Mike needs to know the status of the planned and actual resources. Some of the KPI metrics he uses are machine startup indicators, shutdown indicators, and amount of off-spec product generated.

He uses these to report on the resource capability using assessments of the current mechanical availability of the machines on the fabricating line.

In addition to effectively managing workflow, portfolio managers have another important objective to achieve. They are constantly analyzing portfolio performance and finding ways to improve it. Depending on the industry, organization, or the specific portfolio, other forms of measurement might be needed for complete program-and-project reporting, such as reports concerning key issues in areas such as safety, legal or environmental compliance, and staffing.

But component performance results are only one area to look at; financial reporting is the other major category of reporting. The key performance indicators regarding financial data and perceived value are important criteria used in selecting components and balance of the portfolio.

If a hospital supply company wants to reduce the financial risks associated with carrying new medical devices, they can use the metric of return on investment (ROI) to prioritize potential additions to the portfolio components. Using ROI ensures that the company carries only the devices with the highest financial returns as compared to costs.

Question

Jenny is the fertilizer portfolio manager for an organic gardening supply company. Her company has a new strategic objective to achieve: increasing product placement in existing feed store customers.

Help her distinguish between the types of metrics and reports she can use to manage her portfolio. Not all the examples will have a match.

Options:

A. Metric

B. Report

Targets:

1. The percentage of the quota that has been attained

2. Current product placement compared to last year

3. A schedule for projected sales

4. Net sales increase

5. Seasonal variation in return on investment (ROI)

Answer

This is an example of a metric. Measuring how close you are to your target or quota is in the milestone category of metrics.

This is an example of a report that is relevant to the strategic goal being achieved. Such a report may be generated by metrics and analyzed in comparison to other fiscal periods.

This is not an example of a metric or a report and should not be selected. A schedule is comprised of dates and targets, not measurements or analysis.

This is an example of a metric. A financial measurement such as a sales increase can help determine if the strategic goals are being attained.

This is not an example of a useful metric or report and should not be selected. ROI measures overall return on an initial investment, so determining seasonal variation is not useful.

CHAPTER 2 - Portfolio Management Processes and the Organization

CHAPTER 2 - Portfolio Management Processes and the Organization

Section 1 - Portfolio Management Roles and Processes

Section 1 - Portfolio Management Roles and Processes

By recognizing the importance of understanding how portfolio management processes function within the organization, you are aware of each stakeholder's roles and responsibilities, you understand the forces influencing portfolio management within the organization, and you can help to ensure that the portfolio continues to align with organizational strategy.

In addition, knowledge of the five criteria by which management evaluates the project portfolio during the business cycle helps you prepare to take you place in this evaluation process. These criteria are alignment with corporate strategy; viability of the component, based on key indicators; value in relation to other portfolio components; available resources and portfolio components; and additions and deletions of portfolio components (either projects or programs).

After learning about stakeholder roles and responsibilities, you can understand how those roles

91

inextricably link portfolio management to the organization.

Identifying key stakeholders is critical to the success of your enterprise. And while a stakeholder analysis is a lengthy and difficult process, it is still the best way to identify and ultimately meet stakeholder needs.

"Organizations are driven by a variety of constraints and dynamics brought to bear by the stakeholders. Balancing stakeholders' needs, while staying aligned with strategic goals, is the essence of portfolio management." – The Standard for Portfolio Management

Portfolio management is inextricably linked with the organization. It both influences and is influenced by various forces, including the organizational culture, economic impacts, and organizational impacts.

Understanding portfolio management

Phil is a junior project manager seeking to learn how to do his job well. He's working in an organization in which portfolio management processes are being adopted, and he's not happy about that.

Follow along to learn why Phil is so displeased.

Phil: My job as project manager just got more complicated. I mean, I'm in charge of overseeing projects, but now I'm being told that I have to consider every last person who has anything to do with my projects and everybody else's projects!

Phil is unhappy.

Phil: And I have to think about how other functions affect me. Why can't I just follow the project specs and get on with it?

Phil is really exasperated!

You may feel as Phil does. But, there are many good reasons why you must recognize the importance of understanding how portfolio management processes function within the organization.

This recognition will make you a more valuable team member for the following reasons:

- you will be aware of each stakeholder's roles and responsibilities,
- you will understand the forces influencing portfolio management within the organization,
- you can ensure that the portfolio continues to align with organizational strategy.

Portfolio stakeholders are "individuals and organizations that are actively involved with the portfolio, or those whose interests may be positively or negatively affected because of portfolio management." – The Standard for Portfolio Management

Stakeholders also have powerful positive and negative influences on the portfolio.

Like the PMBOK® Guide, The Standard for Portfolio Management organizes stakeholders into groups and defines roles and responsibilities for the groups. This helps to ensure that key stakeholders are involved in the right ways with portfolio management.

There are many forces that influence portfolio management within an organization. One of the major forces is managers themselves.

Successful portfolio management requires that the organization's managers buy in to the concepts and methods of portfolio management. This buy-in enables them to commit the resources (people and tools) needed for success. It also helps managers to put the interests of the portfolio above those of their own projects, if necessary.

Additionally, it is essential that organizations that adopt portfolio management have a process for handling change.

A well-defined change management process permits portfolio component changes to be handled in a familiar way, along established organizational channels, with appropriate communication to all involved.

One of the most important reasons for you to understand how portfolio management processes function within the organization is that you will be able to take action to ensure that your projects are aligned with organizational strategies.

As a project manager, you know before anyone else whether or not your projects or programs are aligned with organizational strategies, and it's important for you to communicate this information to your managers.

Phil, a junior project manager, is talking with Abe, his mentor, about portfolio management. Follow along as Abe explains the importance of recognizing how portfolio management processes function in the organization.

Abe: Until last year, this organization's project picture was a mess. Each business unit initiated whatever projects it wanted. There was no oversight capability. Resources were always scarce, and nobody really knew how much all this project work was costing us. The new CEO brought in the concept of portfolio management. We worked hard to organize and prioritize our projects according to corporate strategies. Now we can see where the money goes, and where the payoffs are likely to be.

Abe is telling a story.

Phil: Sounds good, Abe. But what does this have to do with me? I want to manage projects, not portfolios.

Phil is slightly puzzled.

Abe: Well, as a project manager in this organization, you're required to understand how portfolio management fits into the business cycle. The executives look at each project as a part of a larger structure. For you to operate efficiently here, you need to be aware of some of these things.

Abe is being persuasive.

Phil: Like what, for example?

Phil is skeptical, but interested.

Abe: For one thing, you need to recognize the importance of understanding stakeholder roles and responsibilities. Stakeholders have enormous power in the project and portfolio management processes. If you make it a point to understand their interests, you'll be better able to appease them, compromise, and meet their objections.

Abe is patiently explaining.

Phil: Stakeholder interests. Check. What else?

Phil is making mental notes. He's fully interested now.

Abe: You need to understand the organizational culture, and the forces that affect portfolio management. For example, in this organization, managers are educated in portfolio management principles. They're all expected to commit to the needs of the portfolio, over and above their own projects.

Abe is explaining.

Phil: That's a tough one. As a project manager, my projects are of paramount importance to me.

Phil is skeptical.

Abe: Understood. But if you're to be successful, you need to recognize that it is important to support the portfolio over your own interests.

Abe is reasoning with Phil.

Abe: The last thing is to understand the importance of aligning all projects with corporate strategies. We evaluate the portfolio at various times throughout the year to ensure that components are in alignment, especially when strategies change. You may find your project canceled or postponed as a result, and you have to be OK with that.

Abe is explaining again.

Phil: Thanks, Abe. This has been a real eye-opener. I knew about portfolio management, of course, but I had no idea it was embedded in the business cycle, or that I would play a large part in it.

Phil has been educated.

After speaking with Abe, Phil recognizes the importance of understanding how portfolio management processes function within the organization. From now on, he will

- be aware of stakeholder roles and responsibilities,
- understand the forces influencing portfolio management within his organization,
- help to ensure that the portfolio continues to align with organizational strategy.

Question

Why is it important to understand how portfolio management processes function within the organization?

Options:

1. To be aware of stakeholder roles and responsibilities
2. To understand the forces influencing portfolio management within an organization

3. To ensure that the portfolio continues to align with organizational strategy

4. To successfully lobby for scarce resources for your own projects

5. To become more successful than your peers at project management

Answer

Option 1: This option is correct. Portfolio management defines roles and responsibilities for key stakeholders. Defined roles and responsibilities are essential for accomplishing portfolio management.

Option 2: This option is correct. When you study the integration of portfolio management processes with the organization, you will understand the organizational forces that affect how portfolios are managed.

Option 3: This option is correct. Once you understand how portfolios are managed in your organization, you will be able to support their alignment with organizational strategy.

Option 4: This option is not correct. Understanding the importance of portfolio management processes in your organization means that you commit to spreading resources across all projects, even to the detriment of your own projects, if necessary.

Option 5: This option is not correct. Understanding the portfolio management processes used in your organization won't necessarily make you a better project manager than your peers, because the processes used for project management are not the same as those used for portfolio management.

Links to corporate strategy

A portfolio of projects and programs is the same in principle as a portfolio of investments. It is "a collection of projects or programs and other work that are grouped together to facilitate effective management of that work to meet strategic business objectives." – The Standard for Portfolio Management

Portfolios contain components. A component is "a constituent part, element, or piece of a complex whole." - PMBOK® Guide

Components can be projects, programs, and even other portfolios. Portfolio components are selected for many reasons, such as to spread risk, to maximize profit potential, or because they represent large investments that need to be monitored closely. Components may relate to each other, but they don't have to.

Organizing components into portfolios gives business executives a "30,000-foot perspective" on the organization's total project load. This perspective is often called a holistic view.

Using the correct project portfolio management processes enables the organization to authorize and prioritize projects, allocate resources appropriately, and monitor projects throughout the project life cycle.

Question

Why do organizations arrange projects into portfolios?

Options:

1. To gain a holistic view of project spread

2. To perform appropriate resource allocation and utilization

3. To monitor projects as investments in order to spread risk and maximize profit potential

4. To ensure that upper management is accountable for project results

5. To ensure that project managers defend their projects' needs over the needs of the portfolio

Answer

Option 1: This option is correct. Grouping projects enables managers to assess them in relation to each other. It is much more difficult to obtain a holistic view of total portfolio performance when projects are viewed in isolation.

Option 2: This option is correct. Viewing projects as a group and assessing their requirements in relation to their performance enables managers to move resources from one project to another, as needed.

Option 3: This option is correct. Portfolio management enables managers to monitor projects as financial investments. Managers monitor risks, as well as costs versus returns.

Option 4: This option is not correct. Accountability isn't the point of portfolio management. Portfolio management facilitates the alignment of an organization's business goals with its projects and programs. It also enables managers to manage projects as investments, maximizing profits and minimizing risk.

Option 5: This option is not correct. Portfolio management is adopted in order to optimize resource utilization, to maximize profits, and to minimize risk. Part of successful adoption of portfolio management is training staff in portfolio theory. One axiom of this theory is subordination of individual project needs to the requirements of the portfolio.

Project portfolio management is a "continuous business process with certain activities invoked during a given year when deemed appropriate by the organization." – The Standard for Portfolio Management

Integrating portfolio management processes into the business cycle helps to ensure that the organization addresses the projects that are most essential to strategy execution and corporate performance.

Follow along to learn about the links between portfolio management processes and the business cycle.

Step 1: The organization's overall strategy is set at the executive level. From this overall strategy, strategic goals and objectives are derived.

The executive level is at the top of the organizational pyramid. It is here that the overall organizational strategy is set.

Step 2: Goals are passed to portfolio managers. Components are selected, prioritized, and approved based on how well they align with goals. Portfolio managers also establish criteria for terminating projects before completion, if necessary.

Goals are passed from the executive level down to the

Step 3: Portfolio managers review the portfolio and balance it, and negotiate agreements with executive managers, operations managers, and program managers.

Step 4: Components that are authorized are passed to Project Portfolio Planning and Management for development. Project managers communicate project status back to portfolio managers at agreed upon intervals.

Step 5: From time to time, portfolio managers are informed of changes to strategies. Portfolio managers review the portfolio to determine whether all components are still aligned. Components that are out of alignment are identified and possibly removed.

For portfolio management purposes, the majority of portfolio additions, changes, and deletions are made during an annual planning process. However, many organizations also plan for quarterly or semiannual portfolio updates.

In addition, whenever corporate strategy changes, there must be a corresponding review of portfolio components. Strategy change often signals the need to add, modify, or remove some components so the portfolio remains aligned.

When management reviews the project portfolio during the business cycle, each component is evaluated in relation to five criteria. These criteria are

• alignment with corporate strategy,

- viability (the ability of benefits to cover costs), as measured by key indicators,
- value in relation to other portfolio components,
- resource availability and portfolio priorities,
- additions and deletions of portfolio components.

Criterion: Alignment with corporate strategy

Corporate strategy answers the questions "Where are we going?" and "How are we going to get there?" Portfolio components are evaluated to ensure that they support the answers to these questions.

During the business cycle, the organization's strategic objectives are reassessed and new ones are established for the coming year.

Portfolio components that help an organization achieve its strategies are validated and approved. New components may be added. If strategies have changed or been abandoned, corresponding projects may be modified or removed.

During annual planning, management of an electric company establishes four new strategies. The portfolio management team examines components of the portfolio to determine how well they support the new strategies.

The team eliminates one project that is no longer valid. Then, the team examines the list of requested projects for the coming year and approves three new projects that align with the new business strategies.

Criterion: Viability according to key indicators

Viability means that a project's benefits outweigh its development costs. Key indicators are metrics that enable management to evaluate cost/benefit performance.

A certain amount of fluctuation in costs is expected during development. However, when project costs spiral upward and outstrip projected benefits, it may be time to end the project. Key indicators, such as total person hours, collected via weekly time sheets, enable management to track project costs during the project life cycle.

A financial company uses the metric return on investment (ROI) to evaluate each project.

After reviewing the portfolio during quarterly assessment meetings, management decided to eliminate two projects because their costs outstrip potential ROI.

Question

When management reviews the project portfolio during the business cycle, each component is evaluated in relation to certain criteria. Match the criteria to examples. Each option may be used more than once.

Options:

A. Viability, according to key indicators

B. Alignment with corporate strategy

Targets:

1. A tire manufacturer pulls the plug on a project to develop a new style of tread. The small market for the product won't cover development costs.

2. A computer manufacturer is expanding into Russia and approves funding for a call center staffed with Russian speakers.

3. Three projects are postponed and one is removed because they no longer support a bicycle manufacturer's business strategy.

Answer

This is an example of evaluating a project's viability, in terms of its costs and benefits. Consumers' tastes are changing, and there is doubt whether the proposed benefits of the project will outweigh costs.

This is an example of aligning portfolio components with corporate strategy. Establishing a call center with a Russian-speaking staff supports the strategy of expanding into Russia.

This is an example of alignment with corporate strategy. Projects must support the business strategy; if they don't, they may be postponed or terminated.

Criterion: A project's value in relation to other portfolio components

Some projects are more important than others in accomplishing strategies and achieving objectives. Portfolio components are prioritized to indicate their importance relative to other portfolio components.

During the business cycle, components are reprioritized. This provides management with an opportunity to reassess project value and possibly reallocate resources as needed.

A textbook publisher adds to its portfolio a program to develop a new science textbook. This program is given top priority; the schedule is tight to meet a state adoption date.

The executive management team agrees that to complete the textbook, resources can be pulled from other projects currently in development. The potential profits from the textbook make this trade-off feasible.

Criterion: Resource availability and portfolio priorities

Like wildfires consume trees, projects consume resources. Portfolio managers must evaluate all projects across the board, to ensure that they do not approve too many projects for the amount of resources they have there are enough resources to accomplish strategic objectives

the most important projects receive critical resources when needed

During a quarterly update of its portfolio, a housewares manufacturer approves three new projects. As part of the approval process, the projected resource utilization figures and schedules are examined to ensure that the projects' needs don't exceed the organization's capacities.

Criterion: Additions and deletions of portfolio components

Portfolio management is strongly linked to benefits management. Adding projects and programs is done in order to maximize the benefits (profits, savings, and risk reduction, for example) that will be realized by the portfolio.

By the same token, components are deleted when their performance is seen to decrease benefits.

A sporting equipment manufacturer selects projects for inclusion in a portfolio based on the risk versus reward equation of each project. This enables the management team to monitor the projects closely and move resources among them appropriately.

Question

During the business cycle, management must review the project portfolio against particular criteria. Match the criteria to examples.

Options:

A. Project's value in relation to other portfolio components

B. Resource availability and portfolio priorities

C. Additions and deletions of portfolio components
Targets:
1. A high-visibility project is in danger of missing its target date. To salvage the project that is in jeopardy, management reassigns programmers from a less important project.
2. A hiring freeze forces management to cancel several low-priority projects that can't be adequately staffed.
3. The portfolio manager for an automotive manufacturer replaces a poorly performing project with a new project that is estimated to bring a large return on investment.
Answer
This is an example of evaluating a project's value in relation to other portfolio components. The high-visibility, important project is given the resources needed to complete it, while the less important project
is made to wait.
This is an example of evaluating resource availability and portfolio priorities. Projects are given resources according to their priorities. Scarcity in personnel resulting from the hiring freeze forces cancellation of several lower-priority projects.
This is an example of additions and deletions of portfolio components. Terminating a poorly performing project and investing that money into a good performer is an important part of portfolio management.
x

Stakeholder analysis

Project work is pervasive in the modern organization. People at all levels are affected by, and involved in, developing, testing, implementing, and deploying projects.

Many of these people have an influence on whether a project is successful or not. The individuals who have an influence on the outcome of project work are called stakeholders.

According to the PMBOK® Guide, stakeholders are "persons and organizations, such as customers, sponsors, performing organizations and the public, that are actively involved in the project, or whose interests may be positively or negatively affected by, execution or completion of the project."

They may also exert influence over the project and its deliverables.

Given that definition, there are hundreds, and possibly thousands, of stakeholders for a project portfolio. Fortunately, not all of them have to be recognized for projects and portfolios to be successful.

There are two types of stakeholders:

key stakeholders

Key stakeholders are individuals and groups that are directly affected by the portfolio and may have a direct influence on it. The commitment and support of key stakeholders is essential for project success.

non-key stakeholders

Non-key stakeholders are individuals and groups that are affected by the portfolio, but who don't need to be recognized for the portfolio to succeed. These stakeholders don't have an influence over the project's success.

Key stakeholders are decision makers and resource suppliers who can have enormous influence on the success of a program, project, or portfolio. For example, people who provide financing, expertise, workers, equipment, and tools are key stakeholders.

Key stakeholders need information about the costs and performance of projects and programs. This enables them to make informed decisions.

Portfolio managers work hard to understand and meet the interests, values, concerns, and objections of key stakeholders. This pays off in the formation of a coalition of support around each project, program, and portfolio.

Ignoring key stakeholder concerns can have severe negative consequences, such as the withholding or delay of funding or critical resources, for example.

Question

Which statements apply to key stakeholders?

Options:

1. Key stakeholders are people and groups who are vitally important for successful portfolio management

2. Key stakeholders require access to cost and performance information for projects and programs

3. Portfolio management is not directly concerned with key stakeholders

4. Key stakeholders are important for project success, but they have nothing to do with portfolio management

Answer

Option 1: This option is correct. Key stakeholders are people and groups whose participation in portfolio management processes is absolutely essential for success.

Option 2: This option is correct. Information on costs and performance enables key stakeholders to make informed decisions and to provide resources when they are needed, for example.

Option 3: This option is incorrect. Portfolio managers work hard to understand the needs and interests of key stakeholders in order to obtain their commitment to portfolio success.

Option 4: This option is incorrect because key stakeholders are the people who provide funding and resources for projects, programs, and portfolios.

Key and non-key stakeholders are identified and their interests are defined through a process called

stakeholder analysis.

Stakeholder analysis is performed during portfolio initiation, to identify the important individuals and groups at the outset; whenever the portfolio is scheduled for updating, in case components change; and whenever there is a change in the stakeholder environment.

Stakeholder analysis can be very complex and time-consuming. However, the payback is huge. The more thorough the stakeholder analysis, the better the support system for the portfolio, and the smoother the workflow. The steps in stakeholder analysis are

identify or review all stakeholders

Brainstorm to identify the people and groups that will affect or be affected by portfolio management processes. Be sure to include groups inside and outside of the organization.

analyze or review the specific interests of each individual or group

Determine the nature of the interest held by each individual or group. Determine whether it is positive or negative.

assess each stakeholder's potential impact on the process

Determine whether the stakeholder is key or non-key. Consider the role the stakeholder will play and whether it will have a negative effect on the project. Rate each stakeholder according to your organization's standards; for example: A (extremely important), B (important), C (not very important).

determine strategies to gain stakeholder support and reduce opposition

Figure out what is required to engage key stakeholders in the project and gain their commitment, and determine how to communicate with them.

After selecting the projects to include in the portfolios, the executive team begins a stakeholder analysis for each portfolio, starting with the portfolio that supports home users. The team performs the following activities:

identifies all stakeholders

The executive team brainstorms and identifies all of the people and groups both inside and outside the company who are affected by the components in the portfolio. The result is a long list of managers, employees, vendors, and customers.

identifies the interests that each stakeholder has in the portfolio

For each stakeholder, the team assesses the exact nature of interest and potential involvement, and whether that involvement is likely to be positive or negative. For example, they find that vendors are particularly interested in the impact of new technologies on the home-user group.

identifies the impact each stakeholder can have on the portfolio

The team rates the importance of each stakeholder's interests. For example, customers are considered A (extremely important) in the home-user portfolio, because without customers' interest, the company's R&D efforts may prove ineffective.

discusses ways to obtain stakeholder commitment

The team discusses ways to obtain stakeholder commitment to portfolio management, and strategies it can use to meet and overcome stakeholder objections and obstacles. The team members decide to set up an online facility to capture interests of stakeholders located outside the company.

In performing a careful stakeholder analysis, the Ringcom team defines its primary support group, determines how to obtain stakeholder commitment, and strategizes how to overcome obstacles to smooth portfolio management.

Question

Sequence the steps in the stakeholder analysis process.

Options:

A. Identify or review all stakeholders

B. Analyze or review the specific interests of each individual or group

C. Assess each stakeholder's potential impact on the portfolio

D. Determine strategies to gain stakeholder support and reduce opposition

Answer

Identify or review all stakeholders is ranked is the first step in the process. Brainstorming to identify or review all stakeholders is the first step in a stakeholder analysis.

Analyze or review the specific interests of each individual or group is ranked is the second step in the process. After stakeholders are identified, the second step the team must take is to determine why and how each individual or group is interested.

Assess each stakeholder's potential impact on the portfolio is ranked is the third step in the process. Evaluating the impact each stakeholder could have on the portfolio is the third step.

Determine strategies to gain stakeholder support and reduce opposition is ranked is the fourth in the process. Strategizing how to gain each stakeholder's commitment or neutralize opposition is the final step in stakeholder analysis.

Stakeholder roles and responsibilities

The level and nature of stakeholder roles and involvement vary from organization to organization and from portfolio to portfolio.

The Standard for Portfolio Management defines 13 stakeholder roles and associated responsibilities. They are executive manager, portfolio manager, program manager, Portfolio Review Board, sponsor, project manager, project team, Project Management Organization, functional manager, operational manager, financial manager, customer, and vendor or business partner.

These 13 roles encompass the requisite functions involved in portfolio management processes in most organizations. But they are not always represented by separate individuals. Though all of the roles are necessary, they may be grouped and performed by fewer people.

Three of the stakeholder roles defined in the Standard for Portfolio Management are concerned with managing the portfolio as a whole:

executive manager

Portfolio Review Board (PRB) portfolio manager

Ringcom Telecommunications is a new player in the wireless communications industry. Ringcom offers a variety of products and packages to both commercial and home users of its services.

The executive team at Ringcom decides to adopt portfolio management. It begins with two portfolios: one for projects that support commercial customers, the other for projects that support home users.

Executive managers are the link between senior managers and portfolio managers. Executive managers communicate strategy information to portfolio managers, and they communicate status information from portfolio managers back to senior managers.

Executive managers are often senior executives themselves. Some executive managers report directly to their company's CEO.

A Portfolio Review Board is like a steering committee for portfolio management. According to The Standard for Portfolio Management, the PRB "dictates the framework, rules, and procedures for making portfolio decisions."

The PRB monitors projects and programs to ensure that they

- maintain their alignment with strategic and operational goals,
- have appropriate resources to deliver the agreed-upon results,
- are effectively sponsored and managed,

116

- have appropriate levels and methods of communication.

The PRB is empowered to make important decisions about the portfolio, such as terminating projects that don't align with organizational strategies or postponing lower-priority projects to free up resources.

Not all organizations have a Portfolio Review Board. Sometimes executive managers perform these portfolio-wide functions instead.

The portfolio manager administers the portfolio. Among her associated responsibilities are

- collecting and assessing performance information on all components,
- assessing how well components are aligned with corporate strategies,
- communicating portfolio status information to the PRB, if one exists, or to executive managers.

It's very important that the portfolio manager have the skills and sensitivity to report bad news to upper- level executives. She must be able to work well with all levels of personnel, including the key stakeholders with whom she communicates.

The executive board of a soft drink company creates a new portfolio to closely monitor its highest-yield but riskiest projects. The board then chooses people to fill important roles.

Executive manager

The board appoints one of its own members to serve as the executive manager for the new portfolio, ensuring a close link between strategy and management of the risky investments.

Portfolio manager

An experienced program manager from the Research and Development Department is appointed to manage the critical resources, as well as oversee the budget and schedule of the projects in the portfolio.

Portfolio Review Board (PRB)

The executive manager sits on a five-member Portfolio Review Board with other executives, including the head of Sales and Marketing. The PRB oversees all of the organization's portfolios and establishes rules and criteria to use for managing them.

Question

A home furnishings store has three product lines: Modern, Traditional, and Contemporary. Each product line is managed as a separate portfolio.

Within the Traditional product line, a new lifestyle collection is being produced, consisting of bedroom, living room, and dining room furniture. Each room will be managed as a separate project.

The executive board meets to discuss how to assign the three roles that link the business needs with portfolio management. Match each role with the appropriate personnel choice.

Options:

A. Executive manager

B. Portfolio manager

C. Portfolio Review Board (PRB)

Targets:

1. Sheila, a senior executive, will be a communications link between the executive management team and management of the Traditional product line.

2. Bill, the vice president of design, is chosen to monitor the development and performance of the Traditional product line.

3. Five senior managers experienced with project and portfolio management are named to an oversight committee. The budget for the new products is submitted to this group for approval.

Answer

The executive manager performs a portfolio monitoring function. She communicates strategy information downward and portfolio management information upward.

The portfolio manager is the individual who administers and manages the portfolio.

A Portfolio Review Board (PRB) is a rule-making entity that oversees portfolio management, including budget approval.

These five portfolio stakeholder roles are concerned with individual portfolio components:

- sponsors,
- program managers,
- project managers,
- project team,
- Program/Project Management Office (PMO).

Sponsors provide the passion and leadership for their projects, programs, or portfolios. They champion their components with upper management and run interference for their project managers. Sponsors are responsible for bringing a component to successful conclusion.

Among their responsibilities are

- removing obstacles, such as conflicts with other projects or programs,
- assisting program managers with formulating business cases used to obtain project funding and approval,
- rewarding project performance to keep motivation high.

Portfolios contain both programs and projects. A program is a collection of related projects. A program manager handles the centralized coordinated management of a program to achieve the program's strategic objectives and benefits. - The Standard for Portfolio Management

Program managers are responsible for

- helping sponsors formulate business cases to obtain funding,
- monitoring project work to ensure products and services are delivered on time and within budget.

The project manager is the individual responsible for achieving project objectives and goals. Typically, project managers are in charge of the planning, execution, tracking, and delivery of their projects. They are responsible for the budget and schedule, and they direct the day-to-day activities of a cross-

functional project team – the people who do the actual project work. In addition to budget and schedule monitoring, project managers monitor project risk and enact risk avoidance and risk prevention measures when needed.

Every project, large and small, should have a project manager.

A project team is a group of workers with the varied skills and abilities necessary to accomplish a project's objectives. In addition to technical knowledge and skills, a project team must also have a good mix of personalities, styles, and intellectual orientations.

Project teams may also include key stakeholders such as customers, vendors, business partners, and representatives from functional areas that supply key resources. Including key stakeholders on a project team enables the project manager to receive timely input and keep everyone informed of status, progress, and plans.

A Program/Project Management Office (PMO) coordinates project and program management activities for components within its domain. A PMO sometimes manages projects related to a single area.

There is overlap among portfolio management, program management, and the functions of a PMO. Be sure to check your organization's procedures to learn how these roles are defined and used in your organization.

The executive team of Unatek Global Game Design is ready to implement a new strategy.

The strategy contains an initiative focused on creating a new adventure-style game for entry into the teen market, and a project to repurpose that game for the school publishing market.

The executive team discusses how the following roles need to be filled in order to implement this strategy with success.

Sponsor

Each project has a sponsor. In addition to ensuring that funding is provided, the sponsors compete with each other to provide motivation to their teams. One sponsor brings a hot dog cart through the department. The other sponsor holds an ice cream social in a conference room. These activities provide a welcome break from stress and allow team members to reconnect on a social level.

Program manager

The vice president for game design is appointed as program manager. This individual makes sure that both projects' schedules are coordinated, and that the projects have the resources they need. She ensures that the projects are defined and integrated into a focused plan of attack.

Program Management Office (PMO)

The PMO, consisting of two senior project managers, oversees the management of both projects in the program, making sure that resources are utilized according to the master schedule.

Project manager

Each project has its own project manager to plan, initiate, monitor, and control the project work. Project managers handle day-to-day development. In addition, they communicate to the program manager on a weekly basis the status of plans, budgets, and schedules.

Project team

Each project has its own project team to carry out its development work. Teams consist of designers, programmers, artists, and testers. Because one project must be nearly completed before the work on the other begins, some of the same people will work on both teams.

Question

Senior managers of the home furnishings store decide that all of the components involved in producing their new collection will be managed as a portfolio.

Each room of furniture is considered a separate program, and within each program are projects for creating new tables, new chairs, and new sofas.

The managers define roles and responsibilities and assign people to fill them. Match each role with an explanation of how the role is filled.

Options:

A. Project team

B. Project managers

C. Sponsor

D. Program managers

E. Program Management Office (PMO)

Targets:

1. Craftsmen are hired for each project

2. Mya, Jon, and Perri are in charge of teams that produce tables, chairs, and sofas, respectively

3. A manager is assigned to each program to motivate team members and help the program managers obtain funding

4. Phil, Don, and Bree manage the projects associated with each room

5. An oversight committee is established to coordinate the work of the project and program managers

Answer

The workers who perform project work and create the products are the project team.

Mya, Jon, and Perri are project managers. They manage the teams and processes that produce the furniture.

Sponsors motivate team members and help to obtain funding. Sponsors champion their components and support development from initiation through to closure.

These three individuals are program managers. Program managers coordinate and manage related projects.

This is an example of a Program Management Office (PMO). The responsibilities of PMOs are determined by the organizations that use them.

These last five roles are concerned with supplying information and resources to portfolio components:

operations managers

Operations managers are the managers from Finance, Human Resources, Marketing, and Corporate Communications. These managers are concerned with day-to-day operations of the organization. They supply resources and often serve as internal customers for projects and programs.

functional managers

Functional managers supervise workers and ensure that their skills are current. Functional managers allocate resources to projects and monitor those resources to ensure that they perform according to plan.

finance managers

Finance managers perform financial analyses on projects and programs and review budget performance. They also help program and project managers to assess budget variances and use statistics and metrics.

customers

Customers are the beneficiaries of project, program, and portfolio management. Customers are the primary drivers for project and program development and supply the critical input to project and product design.

vendors or business partners

Vendors or business partners are key stakeholders because they can influence important functions during project execution.

Sherri is a project manager at Unatek Global Game Design. She oversees a number of projects, including the creation of the new adventure-style game. She manages a cross-functional project team composed of programmers, artists, and instructional designers.

To be successful, her project plan requires the interaction of many key stakeholders.

Functional managers

Functional managers supply the artists, programmers, and instructional designers that comprise Sherri's team. Sherri manages the team and reports back to functional managers about employee behavior and performance.

Operations managers

Producing the final game involves the work of many people throughout the company. For example, marketing will become involved in designing advertising materials for the game.

For this reason, Sherri sends the marketing director copies of appropriate status reports and ensures that the director is kept aware of schedule changes.

Customers

During the beta testing phase, a select group of customers will receive copies of the game for review and testing. Their comments will have a critical impact on the project.

Vendors or business partners

Sherri uses outside vendors for services her company doesn't provide. For example, a vendor is creating a new font for use in the game.

The vendor's cost is a budget item, and the schedule for developing the font is on the critical path for completing the game on time.

Finance manager

Because of increasing governmental regulation, the company's chief financial officer (CFO) is regarded as a key stakeholder on every project.

The CFO must sign off on all formal budget change requests. Sherri also uses the CFO's staff for advice on how to use the prescribed metrics to monitor her project's performance.

To accomplish her project's objectives, Sherri must rely heavily on different business units, groups, and individuals within and outside of her organization.

All of these business units are key stakeholders. While they are only involved sporadically in project work, these stakeholders can have a significant impact on progress and results.

Case Study: Question 1 of 3
Scenario

A television network has heavily invested in project portfolio management. The company maintains separate portfolios for established television shows, pilots, and new shows in development. Close monitoring of portfolios is essential for survival in the competitive world of network TV.

Each pilot and each show in development is managed as a separate project, whereas the established shows are grouped into programs according to type (detective show, sitcom, and drama).

Answer the following questions in order.

Question

The company has well-defined roles and responsibilities. Match each role with a description of the individual or group who fills it.

Options:

A. Executive manager

B. Portfolio manager

C. Portfolio Review Board (PRB)

D. Sponsors

Targets:

1. A senior executive monitors the new shows portfolio and communicates its status to the executive board.

2. A manager oversees the pilot television shows. She collects and assesses performance information on the pilots and passes it to the PRB.

3. This group of five executives has the authority to terminate nonperforming components. At the end of the first business quarter, they cancel two of the pilot shows.

4. For each pilot show there are groups of supporters who help secure continuous funding and ongoing support.

Answer

This describes an executive manager. His responsibilities include communicating strategy from senior management to portfolio managers, and communicating plans and progress from portfolio managers to senior management.

This is a portfolio manager. Her responsibility is to oversee and monitor the performance of all of the components in her portfolio. She communicates with the PRB, or executive management if there is no PRB.

This group of executives is a Portfolio Review Board (PRB). The PRB is granted the authority to evaluate component performance and make important decisions as needed.

Case Study: Question 2 of 3

Match each role with a description of the individual or group who fills it.

Options:

A. Program manager

B. Project manager

C. Program/Project Management Office (PMO) D. Project team

Targets:

1. This manager is in charge of the existing detective shows. He oversees their budgets and schedules to ensure that they are performing as required.

2. This manager is in charge of the planning, execution, tracking, and delivery of one of the pilot shows.

3. This group acts as a resource for project and program management, to obtain additional resources and funding.

4. Producing a pilot requires the efforts of many different groups: camera crews, electricians, stage hands, and onscreen talent.

Answer

This is a program manager. A group of related projects is a program. The program manager is responsible for overseeing the budgets, schedules, and completion of projects within the program.

This is a project manager. The project manager is responsible for overseeing resources and activities required in creating a product.

A PMO can be used for myriad functions to manage projects and programs, including procuring scarce resources and funding.

The workers on a project comprise the project team. The project team is often a cross-functional group of people who report to different functional managers.

Case Study: Question 3 of 3

Match each role with a description of the individual or group who fills it.

Options:

A. Operations manager

B. Functional manager

C. Finance manager

D. Vendor and business partner

Targets:

1. The manager of Human Resources jumps into action to hire a replacement when one of the project managers quits

2. The project manager works through this manager to get the camera crews she needs to produce her shows

3. This manager assists the project manager in deciding how to report budget information to the PRB

4. The project manager contacts this network subsidiary to find out about the availability of New York locations for shooting an episode

Answer

The manager of Human Resources is part of operations management, concerned with the ongoing work of the organization.

The camera crews report to a functional manager. The project manager must work with a functional manager to obtain the resources she needs.

This is a finance manager. Among other responsibilities, finance managers assist project and program managers with reporting on financial matters.

The network subsidiary is a business partner. Business partners are key stakeholders when they can influence project, program, or portfolio management.

Organizational influences

According to a time-worn maxim, the whole is greater than the sum of its parts.

This is certainly true of portfolio management. The value of the portfolio as a whole is greater than the value of its individual components.

Not everyone in an organization appreciates this fact, however. It is often difficult for key stakeholders to accept that the needs of the portfolio must come first, ahead of the needs of their own projects.

A large manufacturing company has plants all over the world. It maintains a large portfolio of programs and projects to support its operations.

One of the company's strategies is to upgrade outdated technology in its foreign plants to put them all on an equal footing and increase their competitiveness in their respective countries. A substantial program is added to the portfolio to accomplish this strategy.

During the second business quarter, the company's earnings stall. The Portfolio Review Board examines the portfolio and determines that a positive financial situation can be maintained by postponing the expensive upgrade program for a third of its plants. This decision, while making the overall portfolio healthier, is extremely unpopular with the affected plant managers.

Follow along as Geoff, the portfolio manager at the manufacturing company, explains the decision to Raj, a plant manager in Pakistan who won't be receiving the upgrades.

Geoff: The company is suffering some serious financial setbacks, and we're having to make some hard decisions. One is to postpone the upgrade project. We'll look at this project again at the start of the next fiscal year. But for now, your operation won't be getting the planned upgrades.

Geoff is sympathetic, explaining the changes to Raj.

Raj: Geoff, that doesn't work for us. How are we supposed to compete with local businesses? Most of them have the latest technology, and they're wiping the floor with us.

Raj is angry.

Geoff: I understand what you're saying. But we must look at the bigger picture. If the financial picture doesn't improve, technology won't matter because many of us won't be here.

Geoff is sympathetic, but he still delivers the bad news.

Raj: I can't make my yearly production goals with the old technology. Raj is quiet as he takes a new tack in the discussion.

Geoff: The good news is that you won't have to. We understand your dilemma, and your goals will be readjusted. You won't have to meet new goals with old tools.

Geoff tries to soothe Raj.

Geoff: I know that it's hard for you to see the benefits of this change. Without it, though, the company could be in serious financial difficulty. That would affect us far more than postponing this project does.

Geoff continues to soothe and rationalize the change to Raj.

Portfolio management is a balancing act. On one side of the scale are stakeholder interests, both long- and short-term interests.

On the other side are the strategic goals of the organization.

The portfolio manager or management team is in the middle, striving to meet stakeholder needs while also meeting organizational goals.

Question

What does the adage, "The whole is greater than the sum of its parts," signify in terms of portfolio management?

Options:

1. Stakeholders should support the requirements of the portfolio above their own projects' needs

2. The value accrued from grouping projects and programs into a portfolio and managing them together outweighs the total value accrued from individual projects and programs

3. The portfolio manager must balance the requirements of the organization with the needs of individual stakeholders

4. The portfolio is worth less than any single project

5. The individual elements of any single project are of primary importance

Answer

Option 1: This option is correct. Stakeholders must understand that their projects and programs are individual investments – only parts of a total investment picture – that can be validated or terminated, according to the organization's goals.

Option 2: This option is correct. The value of individual projects and programs is preserved in the portfolio. However, grouping projects and programs provides the added value of a framework and tools for balancing projects as investments and aligning them with the organization's goals.

Option 3: This option is correct. Portfolio management is a balancing act between stakeholder needs on one side, and organizational goals on the other.

Option 4: This option is not correct. The portfolio is more valuable than any single project, and it's more valuable than a simple collection of projects.

Option 5: This option is not correct. Although each of the elements of any project are important, the value of a portfolio is greater than the sum of its parts, hence the adage.

Portfolio management is inextricably linked with the organization in which it is practiced. It both influences and is influenced by various forces, including three major ones:

- organizational culture,
- economic impact,
- organizational impacts.

Organizational culture is the unique combination of assumptions, values, and behaviors of an organization's individual members.

An organization reveals its culture through outward signs, such as how people dress, how they interact with one another, and how office furniture is arranged, among many other things. There are as many organizational cultures as there are human personality types; they run the gamut from laid back to traditional to fiercely competitive.

One important aspect of organizational culture is the ability to accept change.

All organizations are unique in how resistant they are to change. In order for portfolio management to be implemented successfully, people at all levels of the organization must accept and implement the changes implied by the portfolio.

An organization that has a smoothly functioning change management process is more successful with portfolio management than an organization that does not have such a process.

The change management process provides structure and tools, and lends familiarity to the process and mechanics of change.

For many years, the managers in a global financial management company have managed their own project needs. Any manager could initiate almost any project, with a near guarantee of obtaining funding from the home office.

Things change when the parent company implements portfolio management processes. Managers are expected to submit solid business cases to obtain approval and funding for new projects. It is also expected that managers will cede authority for their individual projects to the portfolio manager.

Not surprisingly, managers regard these changes with suspicion. They are reluctant stakeholders in portfolio management, and have mostly adversarial relationships with the portfolio manager.

Question

What is the most important aspect of organizational culture for the successful implementation of portfolio management?

Options:

1. Ability to compose a good business case
2. Willingness to accept change
3. Willingness to submit to the portfolio manager's will
4. Ability to resist change

Answer

Option 1: This option is not correct. The ability to compose a good business case is important for project and program adoption and funding. However, this ability is a skill, not a part of organizational culture.

Option 2: This option is correct. A willingness to be flexible and accept change is essential to portfolio management. It enables the organization to make the necessary changes that may be required to align projects with organizational goals.

Option 3: This option is not correct. While it is important to recognize the supremacy of the portfolio over individual projects and programs, a willingness to submit to someone's will is not as important as a willingness to accept change.

Option 4: This option is not correct. The opposite is true. The ability to accept change is the most important aspect of organizational culture for the adoption of portfolio management.

A second organizational influence is the economic impact that portfolio management has on an organization's ability to manage its investments.

Two economic impacts that result from grouping projects into a portfolio are that it enables management to

- use the total value of the portfolio as an indicator of investment success or failure,
- balance investments in terms of their risks, rewards, and yields.

Components within the portfolio are treated as individual investments. An organization that wants to achieve aggressive growth and profitability may select a higher percentage of riskier projects. An organization that is undergoing lean times or wants to maintain its current growth may select lower-risk projects.

A portfolio often contains a mix of components: high-risk and low-risk projects, as well as high-yield and low-yield projects. The ideal portfolio mix depends entirely on the organization's strategic goals.

The portfolio of an independent film company contains a mix of projects: four new scripts in development, two projects being storyboarded, one project being filmed on location, and two projects in postproduction.

The project that is being filmed on location is behind schedule, and the rainy season is about to begin. These factors make the project extremely high risk. To prevent further losses, the portfolio manager contacts executive management and recommends shutting down the project. Rain will force additional delays, and the projected earnings from the film won't cover the estimated increase in costs.

Question

What are the economic impacts of portfolio management?

Options:

1. Ability to see projects as investments

2. Ability to populate and manage the portfolio in terms of risks and rewards

3. Ability to use the total value of the portfolio as an indicator of investment success or failure

4. Ability to terminate projects

5. Ability to use business cases as a basis for approving and funding new projects

Answer

Option 1: This option is correct. Projects have costs and benefits, just like investments do. One economic impact of portfolio management is the ability to manage projects according to their costs and proposed benefits.

Option 2: This option is correct. Individual projects have risks and rewards. Projects are chosen for a portfolio based on combinations of risks and rewards that align with the company's goals.

Option 3: This option is correct. It is difficult to know how well investments are doing when they are spread across an organization. Grouping investments into a portfolio enables management to see the total value of the investments.

Option 4: This option is not correct. Portfolio management sometimes involves terminating projects. However, the ability to terminate projects isn't unique to portfolio management.

Option 5: This option is not correct. Business cases are used for approval and funding in many organizations, regardless of whether portfolio management is used.

A portfolio represents the interests of stakeholders throughout an organization. Portfolio management processes can have a significant organizational impact on business processes, rules, the infrastructure and technology, and the organizational structure, for example.

Here are some of the impacts that portfolio management processes can have on an organization:

impact on planning

The requirement of strict alignment between projects and organizational goals is communicated throughout an organization. This helps to ensure that projects that don't align with goals are either not proposed at all, or are terminated early in the proposal process.

impact on organizational structure

The participation of key stakeholders required for effective portfolio management opens new lines of communication across organizational boundaries, produces better cooperation among business units, and effects synergy in portfolio management.

impact on business processes

Portfolio management is only as efficient and effective as the processes and procedures in the business units and functional areas that supply projects and resources. If procedures are ineffective or missing, portfolio management can result in teams doing the wrong things or doing the right things badly.

Effective portfolio management processes in a manufacturing company have beneficial organizational impacts, such as streamlining the project approval process and solidifying a change management process.

This tightening up of processes and procedures results in a more efficient and effective operation, accruing savings that are passed on to the company's customers.

Question

Match each organizational influence with its example.

Options:

A. Organizational impact

B. Organizational culture

C. Economic impact

Targets:

1. Portfolio management processes streamline the organizational processes in a shoe manufacturing company, resulting in increased yearly production.

2. A traditional insurance company's resistance to change delays the successful adoption of portfolio management processes.

3. An oil company organizes projects in portfolios according to their projected earnings. This arrangement enables management to move resources around and maximize ROI.

Answer

The impact of portfolio management on organizational processes can be enormous, resulting in improved processes and increased productivity.

An organization's culture, expressed in its ability to accept change, has a profound effect on both the adoption and success of such new initiatives as portfolio management.

Portfolio management processes have a beneficial economic impact when used to facilitate resource utilization and sustain a good ROI.

Section 2 - Portfolio Management Processes and Process Groups

Section 2 - Portfolio Management Processes and Process Groups

In this overview, you have learned about the benefits of a process-oriented approach and portfolio management: an increased focus on the customer; activities that are organized for profit, rather than based on resource consumption; and ease of integrating the organization's activities with those of other organizations.

In this lesson, you will learn about some criteria for adopting portfolio management processes, and the basic Portfolio Management Process Groups.

In this lesson, you learned about the six conditions that are required for organizations to be successful in implementing portfolio management processes. These are 1) the organization understands and supports portfolio management theory; 2) the organization is projectized; 3) the staff possesses the right skills; 4) project management processes are being used; 5) organizational roles and responsibilities are defined; and 6) a communications plan exists to disseminate business decisions.

Process Groups have some characteristics in common: they are linear; they are linked; and they are iterative.

The Standard for Portfolio Management defines two Process Groups that are essential for successful portfolio management: the Aligning Process Group and the Monitoring and Controlling Process Group.

The Aligning Process Group has seven processes: identification, classification, evaluation, selection, prioritization, portfolio balancing, and authorization. The Monitoring and Controlling Process Group has two processes: portfolio reporting and review, and strategic change.

These Process Groups enable an organization to create, organize, monitor, and control its project portfolios.

A process-oriented approach

A major family-owned toy company operates on the principle, "The squeaky executive gets the grease."

The company funds projects that are proposed by the acknowledged powerful people, who get all the resources they need. The less powerful managers fight for scraps on the fringes. Each executive manages his own roster of projects, hoarding resources to have them available when needed, and making separate deals with a wide variety of suppliers.

There is no project or financial oversight function. Each executive tracks her own projects, but no one keeps track of overall project performance or costs throughout the company.

The result? Disaster! Far more projects are undertaken than there are resources for. Bad ideas get funded without scrutiny. Projects that bog down or stall continue to bleed money when they should be terminated.

The company squanders its precious resources, loses money, and worse, fails to meet customer needs. Everyone recognizes an example of poor management when it is presented to them.

Unfortunately, such scenarios are more common than you might think. Without applying the right management at the right time, it's easy to lose control in a project environment.

To prevent such chaos, many companies adopt a process-oriented approach to portfolio management.

The process-oriented approach has a history of corporate success. Processes establish consistency and standards for what to do, when to do it, and who will do it.

Project management processes are useful in initiating and executing individual projects. However, project management processes aren't adequate in a multi-project environment.

Related projects are often grouped into programs, which are put under the control of a program manager. Then, projects and programs are grouped into portfolios, under the control of a portfolio manager.

While each level of management has prescribed activities for controlling and monitoring projects and programs, it is the portfolio manager who ensures that all the components align with corporate strategies and receive appropriate funding and resources as planned.

Portfolio management processes encompass identifying and authorizing portfolio components and reviewing the status of each individual component, as well as that of the entire portfolio.

When applied correctly, portfolio management processes result in the following benefits:

increased focus on the customer

Projects aligned with corporate strategies are focused on meeting customer needs. Use of cross-functional development teams effects greater efficiency and cost savings, which are passed on to the customer.

activities that are organized for profit, rather than based on resource consumption

Criteria for project funding are determined at the top levels of management. This enables management to assess the estimated costs and potential return on each proposed project. Focus is on the project as an investment and how much profit it will bring.

ease of integrating the organization's activities with those of other organizations

A process approach requires that everyone have the same understanding and use common definitions, making communication much more efficient across department lines and across company lines.

Mismanagement has forced the toy company into receivership. Follow along as Jim, the chief executive officer (CEO), explores solutions with Bridget, the chief financial officer (CFO).

Jim: We've lost track of our customer base. We're funding projects based on people's whims or pipe dreams, with no consideration for what our customers need, or even whether the products will be successful. And the supplier situation! Everybody's got their own suppliers, and you know there's a lot of duplication going on.

Jim is frustrated.

Bridget: Right. We have to do something drastic, and this is the ideal time to do it. I'd like you to think about taking a process-oriented approach to management, and using portfolio management processes to bring the situation under control.

Bridget is stern.

Jim: I'm open to anything at this point. How would it work?

Jim is stern but willing to listen.

Bridget: We need an inventory of all of our projects. Projects that don't support the company strategy must be terminated. You and your officers must meet to determine how you're going to manage the remaining project load, based on your business plan. The ultimate goal is to improve our products and customer relationships, as well as the bottom line. At the same time, we can organize our suppliers and get rid of duplication.

Bridget explains the basics.

Jim: I see. The projects that are left after we clean house will align with our overall strategy, which will improve both our products and our bottom line. This will help make us competitive again and enable us to get our customers back.

Jim is relieved to have a plan.

Bridget: It will take some time to pull this off, but that's the basic idea.

Bridget is pleased.

Jim and Bridget's plan succeeds.

Within a year, the executive board streamlines the project inventory, adopts portfolio management processes, and eliminates duplication in suppliers. The company is reborn: newly focused on the customer and the bottom line.

Best of all, the company begins to turn a profit.

Question

What are the benefits of following portfolio management processes?

Options:

1. You will be more customer-focused

2. You will organize activities in a profit-oriented manner, rather than based on resource consumption

3. You will find it easier to integrate your activities with other organizations

4. You will know how to perform the portfolio manager's roles and responsibilities

5. You will improve your leadership skills

Answer

Option 1: This option is correct. Portfolio management processes remove obstacles and artificial barriers that often hinder project work. Projects that don't align with corporate strategies or benefit customers are not funded, or are canceled.

Option 2: This option is correct. Resource allotments and supplier selection are approved at the portfolio level, so there is no competition at the project level for the resources required to get the work done. This planning optimizes resource utilization, results in selecting the lowest-costing suppliers, and saves money.

Option 3: This option is correct. Processes include specifications for interacting with such external organizations as suppliers. Knowing when and how to integrate project, program, and portfolio activities makes it easier on project managers.

Option 4: This option is not correct. Portfolio managers who direct the execution of these processes are chosen because they already possess such skills. Following the processes does not transfer skills to the individual.

Option 5: This option is not correct. Portfolio management processes are a set of integrated activities that help to manage a collection of projects. They have nothing to do with leadership skills.

Adopting portfolio management processes

The portfolio management processes documented in the Standard for Portfolio Management are a good fit for many portfolios most of the time. Because the processes represent "generally accepted practices," it is agreed that they enhance the probability of success.

However, one size doesn't fit all. Portfolio managers must use their judgment and discretion in deciding which processes to apply and how to apply them. A cookbook approach doesn't work.

The Standard for Portfolio Management makes these assumptions about organizations that wish to use its processes:

the organization already has some form of portfolio management in effect

The Standard for Portfolio Management does not instruct how to manage portfolios. It is a collection of best

150

practices that an organization can use to make its portfolio management processes more efficient and effective, but only if it already has some portfolio management processes in effect.

the organization has a vision and mission statement, as well as a strategic plan, goals, and objectives

The Standard for Portfolio Management covers aligning portfolios with an existing structure of vision, mission, goals, and objectives. Without this structure, the documented processes will not be effective.

It is also assumed that in order to use portfolio management processes successfully, an organization must meet a set of conditions:

- the organization understands and supports portfolio management theory,
- the organization is projectized; that is, a number of projects and programs already exist,
- the staff possesses the skills necessary to manage the portfolio,
- project management processes are being used,
- organizational roles and responsibilities are defined,
- a communications plan exists to disseminate business decisions,

Condition 1: The organization must understand and support portfolio management theory.

Transitioning from a project environment to a portfolio environment requires some big adjustments. Managers at all levels of the organization must understand and buy in to the advantages of managing projects as a group, including changing resource allocations and project priorities as needed. This sometimes means putting the needs of the portfolio above their own project needs.

There must also be a willingness to work cross-functionally to accomplish results rather than to champion one's own department or business unit to the detriment of overall results.

Portfolio management processes will not be effective in an organization in which business leaders don't cede their ability to call the shots or make unilateral decisions.

Condition 2: The organization is projectized; that is, a number of projects and programs already exist.

Portfolio management processes are an umbrella that sits atop project and program management processes. Organizations that don't already use projects and programs as a means to accomplish goals and objectives cannot adopt portfolio management; they don't have the substructure of management processes on which to build.

From another perspective, lumping projects together and calling it a portfolio misses the point. Careful evaluation is required to select projects and programs that minimize risk and maximize profit.

Without a pool of existing projects and programs to choose from, a healthy portfolio cannot be created. Condition 3: The staff must possess the right knowledge and skills to manage the portfolio.

Individuals involved in portfolio management must be able to

understand the organization's strategic plan

To keep projects and the portfolio aligned, portfolio managers must understand how the organization's strategic plan relates to projects and programs.

establish determining factors for managing the portfolio based on the strategic plan

Understanding the organization's plans and goals helps portfolio managers to establish the criteria that are used to categorize and prioritize projects.

consider all of the organization's projects, programs, and other portfolio processes

Knowing the relationships among all of the organization's projects and programs enables portfolio managers to categorize and prioritize components, and assign resources appropriately.

follow agreed-upon processes

Organizations manage portfolios according to the nature and requirements of the business. People involved in portfolio management must agree on using a standard set of processes.

deliver bad news to senior management

Senior managers don't want to hear bad news, but it's essential that they hear the truth. Good communication skills are a requirement.

Often, the skills needed to manage portfolios aren't embodied in one person, so portfolios are managed by teams to obtain the needed mix of skills.

For instance, a portfolio management team might consist of someone proficient with risk management (quantitative and qualitative risk analysis techniques) and another individual who can use statistical analysis techniques. A third team member might calculate and interpret metrics used to assess projects and programs.

Consider the example of several senior managers at a "big box" chain store who think portfolio management might be a good thing for their organization. They accomplish work through projects, so there is a substantial list of projects and programs to choose from.

The managers are also confident they can find individuals with skill sets needed for portfolio management. The managers present their ideas at an executive board meeting, only to find there is little interest among their peer managers, who enjoy the process of competing for scarce organizational resources.

This organization meets two conditions for successful adoption of portfolio management processes, but it does not meet the requirement that everyone must buy in to portfolio management theory.

Question

Which of these situations are favorable for successful adoption of portfolio management processes?

Options:

1. A functional manager within a large organization generates enthusiasm among his peers for adopting portfolio management. Senior management doesn't take notice.

2. An airline company uses projects to accomplish all of the work required to meet its corporate strategies and goals.

3. A midsized telecommunications company spends three months identifying people with the right mix of skills to manage its new portfolio.

4. The operations manager of a tool and die manufacturing company is appointed to the portfolio

management position because it is felt that he knows the most about how the company operates.

Answer

Option 1: This option is not correct. Without the support of senior management, the adoption of portfolio management processes will not happen.

Option 2: This option is correct. A projectized environment is required. Without projects, there can be no portfolio.

Option 3: This option is correct. The right skills are essential for successful portfolio management.

Option 4: This option is not correct. Knowledge of the business is important, but there are far more skills involved in managing the portfolio than knowledge.

Condition 4: Project management processes are already being used.

Portfolio management requires a projectized environment. Within that environment, project management processes are essential for planning and tracking performance, risk management, timely communication and reporting, and resource management, among other things.

With project management processes in effect, portfolio managers can receive the information they require for appropriate resource allocation and risk management.

Condition 5: Organizational roles and responsibilities are defined.

There are a number of functions that must be performed in order for portfolio management processes to run smoothly. The Standard for Portfolio Management defines 13 roles and associated responsibilities for effective portfolio management. They run the gamut from executive manager, portfolio manager, and project manager, to functional managers and vendors.

However, while all of these roles must be performed, they are often combined and performed by a few people, each responsible for several functions.

Condition 6: The organization must have a communications plan for disseminating business decisions.

Information about strategy and changes to business plans must be communicated from senior management to portfolio management in order to allow for correct resource allocation and project prioritization.

Information generated at the project level is elevated to the portfolio management process, where it provides the basis for making portfolio decisions.

Here is an example of a company that displays some of the conditions required for successful portfolio management. A manufacturing organization has a strong network of project managers, through which it manages its projects and programs. It also has well-defined roles and responsibilities.

When the corporation adopts portfolio management processes, it creates a portfolio management team. An executive manager is designated as the point person for communicating business plans to portfolio management.

Portfolio management distributes the appropriate information to project managers. They in turn communicate it to their teams, which include project sponsors, and functional and operations managers.

The line of communication flows from executive managers down through the organization, and from the organization back up to executive managers.

The line of communication flows from executive management to portfolio management and down through the organization, and from the organization back up to executive management.

Question

Which of these situations are favorable for the organization's successful adoption of portfolio management processes?

Options:

1. A small fashion house creates custom designs and is not organized into projects.

2. A water purifying plant has defined roles and responsibilities for project, program, and portfolio management.

3. A jewelry manufacturer organized each line of jewelry into programs. New items are treated as separate projects.

4. A small reinsurance company has no formal communications plan.

Answer

Option 1: This option is not correct. An organization should be projectized if it is to adopt portfolio management processes. A base of project management processes provides a structure on which to build.

Option 2: This option is correct. Defined roles and responsibilities are essential because they define who does what tasks and when tasks are performed.

Option 3: This option is correct. A projectized environment is conductive to adopting portfolio management processes.

Option 4: This option is not correct. A communications plan is essential to the adoption of portfolio management.

Everyone must be aware of the status of business goals and strategies, so that they can keep their projects and programs aligned.

Here is an example of an organization assessing its readiness for portfolio management.

MyBudget Software has a history of success with project management processes, and now the executive board members are eager to adopt portfolio management. They feel that pairing strong project management with a proven method for directing limited resources toward projects that are achievable and strategically aligned with business goals will give them an unbeatable advantage in the marketplace.

Project management processes require well-defined roles and responsibilities, which MyBudget Software has. The company also has a good communications plan, which it can build on when portfolio management is added.

The board puts together a team to investigate the probability of success with portfolio management.

Follow along as Alexis and Tim discuss whether MyBudget Software meets the conditions for implementing portfolio management processes.

Alexis: I think we've got our ducks in a row. The biggest obstacle was getting managers to buy in to portfolio theory...the whole idea that the collection of projects is the important thing, not each manager's individual projects.

Alexis is explaining.

Tim: That's right. If the executives are going to keep fighting over resources and project priorities, we'll never get anywhere! I think they get it now. The training programs and seminars have been helpful.

Alexis: We have a projectized organization and a history of success in meeting schedules and budgets through strong project management. And we already have roles and responsibilities defined. All we need to do is add the new roles and responsibilities required for portfolio management.

Tim: Right. And our strong project management base provides a foundation for communicating our business plans throughout the company. Once we're established, the portfolio management team will be the clearinghouse for information: from executive managers to the project teams, and from the project teams back up to executive managers.

Alexis: The one thing we might be lacking is the skills piece. We need to think about the skills and abilities that will be required to manage our portfolio, and then determine who in the organization has those skills.

Tim: Agreed. This will be our priority. We have enough information and structure in place to make a beginning with portfolio management processes. But over the next few months, we'll need to find or hire people who possess the skills we need to manage our portfolio.

Alexis and Tim determine that their organization meets most of the conditions for adopting portfolio management processes: support from management, a projectized organization, entrenched project management processes, a basis for creating a communications plan, and well-defined roles and responsibilities.

The one criterion they don't meet is having the skills required for portfolio management. Now, they must determine how to obtain those skills.

Case Study: Question 1 of 2

Scenario

For your convenience, the case study is repeated with each question.

An online recruitment agency, Quick 24x7, was founded in July, 2000. It has head offices in Seattle, Washington, and Bangalore, India, and has regional offices in New York, Dublin, Frankfurt, and Milan. The company employs 1,300 people worldwide.

The company is considering portfolio management. Answer the questions that follow in any order.

Question

Which of the conditions found at Quick 24x7 are favorable for adopting portfolio management processes?

Options:

1. The company has a solid communications plan that ensures business decisions are communicated to all head offices via the company intranet, e-mail, and a newsletter

2. The environment is heavily project oriented, with projects ranging from creating an international, rather than local, web site, to training staff in recruitment techniques

3. Project management processes are being followed strictly throughout the organization

4. There is no portfolio management knowledge or skill base in the organization, but senior management

has many bright, experienced people

5. The CEO of the Indian subsidiary was once a senior project manager and wants to acquire portfolio management skills

Answer

Option 1: This option is correct. One of the conditions for the adoption of portfolio management is a good communications plan for disseminating business information throughout the organization.

Option 2: This option is correct. Portfolio components are projects and programs. Without projects, there can be no portfolio.

Option 3: This option is correct. Project management processes provide the framework for managing, controlling, and communicating project information to and from portfolio management.

Option 4: This option is not correct. Successful portfolio management requires a unique skill set, as well as knowledge of business plans. A lack of skills is unfavorable for portfolio management.

Option 5: This option is not correct. Prior experience with project management is not one of the criteria for successful adoption of portfolio management.

Case Study: Question 2 of 2

Which of these conditions are favorable for the successful adoption of portfolio management processes at Quick 24x7?

Options:

1. The management teams at all head offices are trained in portfolio management theory

2. Portfolio management roles and responsibilities, such as executive manager, portfolio manager, and

   project manager, are clearly defined

3. Management at one of the offices seems to be indifferent to portfolio management

4. The organization is successful, large, and has offices throughout the world

5. The executive board intends to hire people with the requisite portfolio management skills

Answer

Option 1: This option is correct. For a company to be successful in adopting portfolio management, everyone must understand portfolio management theory.

Option 2: This option is correct. Roles and responsibilities must be defined in order to ensure a smooth adoption and execution of portfolio management processes.

Option 3: This option is not correct. For portfolio management to succeed, managers must buy in to portfolio management theory.

Option 4: This option is not correct. The size of an organization and its structure have no bearing on whether the organization will be successful adopting portfolio management processes.

Option 5: This option is correct. Having the right skills is essential for the successful adoption of portfolio management.

Characteristics of Process Groups

People often complain about routine, equating the routine with the mundane and boring.

However, without routine, people would have to figure out how to do the same things over and over again, every day. Very little progress would ever be made. Besides, there is comfort in knowing that one can obtain the same results by performing the same tasks in the same way.

In business, another word for "routine" is "process." Processes depend on doing the same things in the same way, every time.

Processes are organized into Process Groups. A Process Group is a collection of related processes that work together to achieve business objectives.

The processes documented in the PMI® standards for project, program, and portfolio management share some characteristics. For example, processes are

linear

Processes are performed in a defined order, according to clear dependencies.

linked

The output of one Process Group is the input to the next Process Group.

iterative

The characteristics of Process Groups are illustrated by the way in which the five Project Management Process Groups interrelate.

Linear

The five Project Management Process Groups are arranged vertically. The arrows between them reflect the order in which they are performed and the direction of the output flow. It's important that activities are in the prescribed order because many activities build on each other.

Linked

Each Process Group links to the Process Group below it and the one above it. Outputs from each Process Group are inputs to succeeding Process Groups. For example, the Planning Process Group requires creating a project plan. The project plan, an output, serves as an input to the remaining Process Groups.

Iterative

Arrows on the right of the diagram indicate that there are iterations, or loops, within and among the Process Groups. For example, during the Executing Process Group, it's often necessary to perform activities from the Planning Process Group.

Philippa is a project manager at Unatek Global Game Design. She is leading a new, high-visibility project.

Observe how Philippa explains the characteristics of Project Management Process Groups to her project team members.

Philippa: On this project, we're going to follow the Project Management Process Groups. These Process Groups document what activities to do, when to do them, and who should be involved. This will give us the guidance to develop the games in the most efficient and effective way possible.

Philippa: The five Process Groups are linear; they are performed in a particular order because they build on each other. For example, when we're finished with the Initiation Process Group, we'll know the project's scope and objectives, which is essential information for the Planning Process Group.

Philippa: Process Groups are linked; the outputs of one Process Group serve as inputs to subsequent Process Groups. The project management plan for each game, produced during the Planning Process Group, is used by all subsequent Process Groups.

Philippa: Another important characteristic of Process Groups is that they are iterative. For example, on my last project we didn't realize how overly aggressive the schedule was until we'd finished the Planning Process Group. When we did realize the risks to the schedule, we repeated the risk management processes and updated the project management plan. These loops occur throughout the project life cycle.

Philippa: Project Management Process Groups represent best practices that people have employed over many years in getting projects done. They're tried and true, and offer us the best chance of success in the development of our new games portfolio!

Now that Philippa has finished her explanation, she is confident that her project team members understand the shared characteristics of the Process Groups.

Question
What are the characteristics of Process Groups?

The graphic is a flow diagram of the five Project Management Process Groups. Each Process Group is in a separate block, in a specified order, one below the other. Arrows on the outside of the diagram indicate some Process Groups reach back to perform activities and processes in other Process Groups.

Options:
1. Linked
2. Linear
3. Iterative
4. Cookbook approach
5. Required

Answer

Option 1: This option is correct. The output of one Process Group is the input to the next Process Group.

Option 2: This option is correct. Processes are performed in a defined order, according to clear dependencies.

Option 3: This option is correct. Processes are often performed over and over again, in loops.

Option 4: This option is not correct. There is nothing cookbook about the Process Groups. Project managers decide which processes and Process Groups will be used for any given project.

Option 5: This option is not correct. Project managers determine which Process Groups and processes will be used in the development of any project.

The Portfolio Management Process Groups

The Standard for Portfolio Management defines two Process Groups that are essential for successful portfolio management:

Aligning Process Group

The Aligning Process Group is concerned with adding the right projects to the portfolio and balancing the mix of components to ensure that organizational goals are met.

Monitoring and Controlling Process Group

The Monitoring and Controlling Process Group reviews performance indicators periodically to ensure continued alignment with strategic objectives and appropriate resource utilization.

Both Process Groups rely on an organization's existing business processes. For example, as new projects are planned and executed according to regular business processes, data is sent to the portfolio manager for analysis. The portfolio manager uses the analysis plus portfolio management processes to control and improve portfolio results through the organization's existing management resources.

Sharing information and processes helps to ensure a tight linkage between business processes and portfolio management. It ensures that accurate and timely information is always available for decision- making.

The Aligning Process Group contains seven processes:

identification

The identification process gathers current information on projects and programs, and then creates an inventory of ongoing and new components for possible inclusion in the portfolio.

categorization

Using the inventory from the Identification process, the categorization process assesses components and groups them according to criteria that are based on the strategic plan. Categorization helps the team to see whether and how these components align with strategic plans.

evaluation

Using output from the categorization process, the evaluation process gathers current qualitative and quantitative information about each component and evaluates its suitability for inclusion in the portfolio.

selection

The selection process uses results from the evaluation process, as well as selection criteria derived from the strategic plan, to create a short list of components to be considered for portfolio inclusion.

prioritization

The prioritization process assigns weights to components within each category, based on business goals. Priorities are used to determine which components are the most important and should receive required resources.

portfolio balancing

The portfolio balancing process develops the mix of portfolio components that has the best potential for supporting the organization's strategies and achieving its business objectives.

authorization

The authorization process formally allocates resources to the selected portfolio components.

Processes within the Aligning Process Group are performed when the organization first establishes its portfolio and when it reviews its business goals, usually during the annual budgeting process.

The processes are also used on an as-needed basis, when business goals or strategies are refreshed or changed.

The processes in the Aligning Process Group ensure that the right amount of analysis and communication occurs so that the correct actions can be taken on potential portfolio components.

Question Set

There are seven processes within the Aligning Process Group.

Question 1 of 2

Question

Match each process with its description.

Options:

A. Identification

B. Categorization
C. Evaluation
D. Selection
Targets:
1. Create a list of projects and programs
2. Group components by business strategy
3. Assess each component's suitability for the portfolio
4. Choose components for inclusion
Answer
An inventory of all projects and programs is compiled during the identification process.

After an inventory is compiled, the categorization process groups projects and programs according to categories that correspond with business strategies.

During the evaluation process, categorized projects and programs are evaluated to determine which are suitable for inclusion in the portfolio.

Components are chosen for inclusion in the portfolio.
Question 2 of 2
Question
Match each process with its description.
Options:
A. Prioritization
B. Portfolio balancing
C. Authorization
Targets:
1. Rank components within categories
2. Review components to insure there is the optimum mix for achieving business objectives
3. Obtain funding and resources
Answer

After selection, prioritization occurs, during which projects and programs are prioritized within their categories, according to predefined criteria (cost, size, and benefits, for example).

Portfolio balancing includes activities that create the best mix of components for achieving business objectives.

Components are submitted for authorization for funding and resource allocation, during the authorization process.

The second Process Group in portfolio management is the Monitoring and Controlling Process Group.

This Process Group is designed to "ensure that the portfolio as a whole is performing to predefined metrics determined by the organization." - The Standard for Portfolio Management

To achieve its purpose, the Monitoring and Controlling Process Group uses two processes:

portfolio reporting and review

During the portfolio reporting and review process, reports on performance indicators are gathered, and the portfolio is reviewed at scheduled intervals to ensure that alignment is maintained and resources are properly utilized.

strategic change

During the strategic change process, the reports produced by the portfolio reporting and review process are used to determine when and how to respond to strategic changes in order to keep the portfolio healthy and balanced.

Reviews are performed on a scheduled basis, and may be done in multiple iterations to examine the portfolio from different perspectives (benefits, risks, and costs, for example).

Reviews provide managers with information that enables them to see the effects their decisions have had on the portfolio and its return on investment (ROI). An annual review cycle captures all decision-making and its impact on the portfolio and its ROI over time. It also reveals how market changes, customer demands, and company policies have affected the portfolio.

When changes are required, the strategic change process often reaches back to processes in the Aligning Process Group, in order to add, change, or delete components as needed to maintain the portfolio balance.

Question

Match each process with its descriptions. Each option may be used more than once.

Options:

A. Portfolio reporting and review B. Strategic change

Targets:

1. Gather and report on performance indicators
2. Respond to changes that affect the portfolio
3. Review the portfolio at scheduled intervals to ensure alignment is maintained
4. Review the portfolio to ensure resources are properly utilized

Answer

This is a description of portfolio reporting and review. Information on performance indicators is gathered to enable managers to assess the portfolio's performance.

This is a description of the strategic change process. When business strategies change, it is often necessary to make changes to portfolio components.

This is a description of the portfolio reporting and review process. Monitoring is essential for maintaining alignment with business objectives.

This is a description of the portfolio reporting and review process. Resources are always scarce, so proper allotment and utilization are essential.

CHAPTER 3 - Portfolio Management Process Groups

CHAPTER 3 - Portfolio Management Process Groups

Section 1 - The Aligning Process Group

Section 1 - The Aligning Process Group

This lesson explains the basic activities, the tools and techniques, and the inputs and outputs associated with the processes of the Aligning Process Group.

Identification of components is the first step in aligning the elements of a portfolio. To qualify for inclusion in the portfolio, components must meet the requirements of the component definition and have all necessary key descriptor information.

The up-to-date list of identified components that this process provides is the basis for all subsequent alignment processes.

The Categorization process takes a list of identified components and sorts them into unique categories so that they can be compared meaningfully.

The subsequent Evaluation process takes the categorized components and gives them a value – a score – that can be used for comparison, and later for selection, prioritization, and balancing.

The scores and other information from the Evaluation process are used in the Selection process to narrow the list of components by considering them in relation to organizational capacities.

That narrowed list of valuable components is then put in order of importance in the subsequent Prioritization process using one or more of the criteria scoring models.

The Portfolio Balancing process works to determine the optimum portfolio component mix – one that maximizes returns and best supports the organization's strategic initiatives. By ensuring that resource planning and resource allocation are tied to company strategy, the Portfolio Balancing process maximizes possible portfolio returns while taking factors such as risk into account.

The Authorization process is the action step that follows balancing. It formally authorizes funds for developing the selected components and also communicates all portfolio balancing decisions.

Overview of aligning processes

Things change. It is a fact of life and most certainly a fact of project and portfolio management.

In turbulent times, Abraham Lincoln once said "The dogmas of the quiet past are inadequate to the stormy present." When dealing with portfolio management, the best laid management plans can become "dogmas of the past" unless they are monitored and occasionally re-evaluated.

The Aligning Process Group ensures that portfolio management considers strategic alignment throughout the various aligning processes. But after project authorization, the business environment begins to have its effect. As projects and programs get underway, scope may start to creep, budgets may be exceeded, or milestones missed.

Even positive changes – such as greater than expected returns or coming in under budget – can have effects on the portfolio that require adjustments to be made for optimum performance. Larger adjustments may be needed if major changes come at a strategic level.

The Monitoring and Controlling Process Group reviews performance indicators to assure continued alignment with organizational strategy and the most effective use of resources.

The kinds of variations that you may have observed in your own projects are precisely the changes the Monitoring and Controlling Process Group deals with across a portfolio.

The Monitoring and Controlling Process Group is responsible for two processes:
- the Portfolio Reporting and Review,
- process the Strategic Change process.

The Portfolio Reporting and Review process involves gathering and reporting on performance indicators, periodically re-examining the portfolio. Using this process verifies that the portfolio contains only the components that best support the achievement of the strategic goals and that resources are used effectively.

Feedback from various projects and programs is used for monitoring. Information about progress against the portfolio plan, financial results, performance against competitors, customer satisfaction, resource usage, budget usage, and many other factors, is used.

The review process also involves considering performance at the portfolio level, based on characteristics such as portfolio management criteria, dependencies, risk, and financial performance.

It's important to understand the Monitoring and Controlling Process Group because you'll be able to

respond to changes in strategy

The Strategic Change process tracks and integrates changes so portfolio management can respond. The organization can address new business conditions, measure their effect, and take action.

ensure that resources are used effectively

The Portfolio Reporting and Review process involves periodically monitoring resource usage. This ensures that, as the environment changes, the portfolio mix continues to make the best use of resources.

ensure that performance expectations are met

By monitoring characteristics such as performance against the plan, financial performance, and scope creep, the Portfolio Reporting and Review process ensures that delays or poorer returns are adjusted for in time to keep performance on track. Re-evaluating the criteria and metrics used for tracking is also part of the process.

The Portfolio Reporting and Review process can provide direction to project or program managers or component rebalancing recommendations to portfolio management.

It can also make upward recommendations to organizational management as to needed changes in the strategic plan, to the component selection criteria or metrics, or to the portfolio review process itself.

The other process of the Monitoring and Controlling Process Group is the Strategic Change process, which enables portfolio management to respond to changes in strategy.

Small changes to strategy may not require changes to the portfolio. But significant changes may impact the portfolio because the strategic plan is the basis for all alignment processes – such as identification, categorization, and prioritization. Larger strategic changes may result from new leadership wanting to adjust organizational strategy according to different goals, or from market variations that require changes in profit thresholds.

As the environment changes – internally or externally – the organization may also decide to change the criteria used to determine the composition and direction of the portfolio.

The New Product portfolio for a natural foods company benefited greatly from the review of key performance indicators associated with the processes of the Monitoring and Controlling Process Group.

Portfolio Reporting and Review process

The tools used in the Portfolio Reporting and Review process indicated that certain portfolio components weren't performing as expected. Although the portfolio as a whole was performing well, the Schedule Performance Index (SPI) for both the USDA Compliance program and the New-products Training program indicated both were severely out of line with projections.

Since budget-usage indicators showed the Product Development program was running 30% under budget, those funds were reallocated to the delinquent projects to get them back on schedule. The portfolio was rebalanced for a more effective use of resources.

Strategic Change process

The Strategic Change process recently came into play when the company was acquired by a larger corporation. The new parent corporation has a much greater emphasis on controlling risk.

Using the tools of the Strategic Change process, the strategic plan was altered slightly to better align with the new direction. This resulted in revised component definitions and three new measurements for risk assessment being added to the component Evaluation process. A basic change in strategy was quickly and appropriately incorporated.

Question

Why is understanding the Monitoring and Controlling Process Group important?

Options:

1. You will be able to respond to changes in strategy quickly and appropriately

2. You will be able to ensure that resources are used effectively

3. You will be able to start with the portfolio component mix that best supports the organization's strategic goals

4. You will be able to monitor performance and prevent strategic change from occurring

5. You will be able to ensure that performance expectations are met

Answer

Option 1: This is a correct option. The Strategic Change process tracks and takes into account strategic changes to enable portfolio management to respond appropriately.

Option 2: This is a correct option. Even carefully aligned portfolio components typically require adjustment once work begins. For example, environmental factors such as changes in markets can affect predicted component returns and results.

Option 3: This is an incorrect option. The Aligning Process Group works to design the initial component mix. The Monitoring and Controlling Process Group comes into play after work has already begun to ensure continued alignment and optimization.

Option 4: This is an incorrect option. The Monitoring and Controlling Process Group does not prevent strategic change from happening, but rather allows strategic change to occur and enables portfolio management to respond appropriately.

Option 5: This is a correct option. By carefully monitoring actual component performance from a variety of perspectives, adjustments can be made to components, to the portfolio mix, or to the metrics used to measure performance – ensuring goals are met.

Identifying components

The same questions that apply to managing an investment portfolio of stocks, bonds, real estate, and so forth, apply to managing a business portfolio made up of various projects, subportfolios, programs, or other work.

Every component of a portfolio is, in effect, an investment – of time, resources, effort, and money. The first question in managing these investments is: "What items make up my portfolio?"

Identification of components is the first process of the Aligning Process Group. The Identification process works to develop an up-to-date list, with accompanying information, of all components – both current and proposed – that will be managed as part of a given portfolio.

To identify qualifying components, the Identification process requires certain inputs: the organization's strategic plan

- the component definitions,
- key descriptor information,
- an inventory of existing and proposed components.

The organization's strategic plan – including its mission statement, long-term goals, objectives, and the means available to achieve them – is needed to develop a component definition. A preliminary comparison of all inventoried components to the component definition is used to eliminate those that do not qualify to be part of the portfolio.

For example, a given strategic plan might call for rapid growth and expansion into foreign markets. The resulting component definition for a portfolio might then require that all components show 25% annual growth and that they open up one new foreign market per year.

Key descriptors are the characteristics used throughout the alignment process to qualify, select, evaluate, and eventually authorize the components of a portfolio. As such, they must accompany the selected components throughout the process.

Requirements are defined and acceptance levels are set for filtering out unacceptable components.

The person or department promoting the inclusion of a given component must supply complete key descriptor information so the portfolio manager has a common basis for comparison. Missing key descriptor information means rejection from the portfolio.

The portfolio managers for Byron Air, a major airline company, are required to consider administrative costs, resource usage, and financial expectations for all portfolios. Therefore, all portfolio components must have adequate information for the following key descriptors: component number, component description, class of component, market risk level estimates, key stakeholders, resources required, return on investment, and budget estimates.

The company uses experts to assess any technical and management details, as well as the inputs needed.

Question

For the Identification process to qualify components, it requires certain inputs.

What are the inputs to the Identification process?

Options:

1. Key descriptors
2. Strategic plan
3. Component definitions
4. Inventory of existing components
5. Inventory of proposed components
6. A prioritized list of key descriptors
7. Inventory of previously removed components

Answer

Option 1: This is a correct option. Key descriptors are predefined and an acceptable level is set for each. They will later be required for categorizing and evaluating the selected components.

Option 2: This is a correct option. The strategic plan is the basis for all decisions related to portfolio management and is used to develop the component definitions.

Option 3: This is a correct option. Component definitions are based on the objectives set out in the strategic plan and are useful for initial screening.

Option 4: This is a correct option. This is a list of previously authorized components that are reviewed to ensure they should continue to be included in the portfolio.

Option 5: This is a correct option. Proposed components are examined in the same way existing components are to decide if they should be included or rejected.

Option 6: This is an incorrect option. The key descriptor information is an input to the Identification process but descriptors are not prioritized.

Option 7: This is an incorrect option. Unless these previously removed components have some relevance to the current portfolio – that is, they have been reworked and proposed for inclusion – they are not needed here.

Using the component definition and the key descriptor data, the Identification process checks ongoing components to be sure that they are still aligned to the strategic plan and are still qualified to be part of the portfolio. Proposed components must also face the same test to see if they should be included or rejected. Components that do not fit the definition are removed.

The identified valid components are also sorted into predetermined classes – typically as project, program, sub-portfolio, or other works.

The outputs of the Identification process are

a list of qualifying components including key descriptor information

This is a list of all components that meets the definition. In addition to key descriptor data, the list may include documentation regarding relationships among the various components. This information will be used during subsequent alignment processes for categorizing, evaluating, and selecting components.

a list of rejected components including key descriptor information

A list of rejected components – including their detailed key descriptor information – is necessary since some of these may be reworked and resubmitted, while others may be directed elsewhere.

Lars is a portfolio manager for Brocadero, an international manufacturer and seller of hi-fi and public-address equipment for businesses. He is engaged in identifying the components of his portfolio.

Based on Brocadero's company vision, the stated company mission is "to provide quality economical audio equipment sales and service to business users." This has resulted in three strategic goals: improve the quality of the product range; reduce the cost to the consumer; and generate annual business growth of more than 10%.

Based on the three strategic goals, the component definition for the New Product portfolio has been stated as: "Must show either an increase in revenue of 10% or an increase in quality of 10% while maintaining or reducing costs." To qualify the components, key descriptor information must include new revenue expectations, project milestones, quality impact, and cost reduction.

Component A – MegaBass PA system

188

The MegaBass PA new product project is expected to increase revenue by 9%, with no effect on quality and no effect on cost. Project milestones are provided.

Component B – UltraBass PA system

The UltraBass PA is a development project that is expected to increase revenue by 15%, have a cost decrease of 40%, and a quality improvement of 30%. Project milestones are provided.

Component C – PortaBass conference system

The PortaBass conference system project is expected to increase revenue by 15%, have a cost increase of 11%, and a quality improvement of 20%. Project milestones are provided.

Component D – SupremeBass entertainment system

The SupremeBass new product project is expected to increase revenue by 12%, have a cost decrease of 13%, and a quality improvement of 18%. Project milestones are not available.

Component E – New Product marketing program

This marketing program is expected to increase revenue by 32%, a cost decrease of 5%, and a quality improvement of 19%. Project milestones are provided.

After examining the available key descriptor information, Lars discusses the components with his assistant, Ellen.

Ellen: All the product development areas of the company have put forth their candidates for the New Product portfolio. In addition, the Marketing Department has submitted a program it believes should be included.

Lars: Based on the company's strategic plan, the component definition for this portfolio calls for all projects to show an increase in either revenue or quality of 10% annually while maintaining or reducing cost.

Ellen: So judging by the key descriptor information each department gave us, the MegaBass PA system won't meet either the revenue or the quality requirements.

Lars: That's right. And of the four components that do meet the first qualification, only three meet the other requirement of the definition – to at least maintain current costs.

Ellen: I see that the PortaBass conference system – Component C – will result in an 11% increase in cost, so that's why we need to reject it.

Lars: Also, since the sponsor of the SupremeBass entertainment system failed to provide key descriptor information for milestones, this component has to be rejected as well.

Lars used the component definition and the key descriptor information to output a list of the two qualifying components – the UltraBass PA system and the marketing program. Their associated key descriptor information is included.

Lars rejected a project that would have led to increased cost – it can be reworked for possible inclusion in the New Product portfolio next quarter. The rejected SupremeBass entertainment system project will have to be resubmitted with more complete key descriptor information.

This list of rejected components – components A, C, and D – makes up the second output of the process, and must also include the associated key descriptor information.

Case Study: Question 1 of 3

Scenario

For your convenience, the case study is repeated with each question.

The Human Resources Department of Mariner Computer Solutions, an IT consultancy firm, has a training division organized by the type of training.

As the IT Training portfolio manager, your portfolio contains a number of ongoing courses, and you are constantly being called upon to develop new courses to support the IT function.

Question

Which components meet the component definition?

Options:

1. Component #1– Intro to IT
2. Component #2 – Intermediate IT
3. Component #3 – Advanced IT
4. Component #4 – History of IT
5. Component #5 – Training Delivery System

Answer

Option 1: This is a correct option. The Intro to IT course is useful as a prelude to other courses, adequately diverse, and sufficiently up to date.

Option 2: This is an incorrect option. The Intermediate IT course is useful and sufficiently up to date, but no longer meets the diversity requirement of the component definition.

Option 3: This is a correct option. The Advanced IT course is in demand, sufficiently up to date, and sufficiently diverse.

Option 4: This is an incorrect option. The History of IT course is not useful, even though it satisfies the other conditions of the component definition.

Option 5: This is a correct option. The Training Delivery System satisfies the requirement for a useful component, it is up to date and sufficiently diverse.

Case Study: Question 2 of 3

Which of the components that meet the component definition fail to meet the key descriptor requirements?

Options:

1. Component #1– Intro to IT
2. Component #3 – Advanced IT
3. Component #5 –Training Delivery System

Answer

Option 1: This is an incorrect option. Key descriptor information, including name and number, ratio of minority/women images, most recent update information, and budget amount, has been included.

Option 2: This is a correct option. Although this course meets the component definition, there is missing key descriptor information, since no budgetary information has been provided by the sponsoring department.

Option 3: This is an incorrect option. All key descriptor information is present.

Case Study: Question 3 of 3

What are the outputs of the Identification process for the IT Training portfolio?

Options:

1. A list of qualifying components that includes components 1 and 5 with associated key descriptor information

2. A list of rejected components that includes components 2, 3, and 4 with associated key descriptor information

3. A list of qualifying components including components 1, 3, and 5 with associated key descriptor information

4. A list of rejected components including components 2 and 4 with associated key descriptor information

Answer

Option 1: This is a correct option. These two components are the only two that qualify as part of the scenario since they meet the component definition and they have complete key descriptor information.

Option 2: This is a correct option. The rejected component list – including components that failed to meet the definition and lacked key descriptor information – is an important output of the Identification process and must include the associated key descriptor information.

Option 3: This is an incorrect option. Component #3, the Advanced IT course, had insufficient key descriptor information and should not be included in the list of qualified components.

Option 4: This is an incorrect option. Component #3, the Advanced IT course, had insufficient key descriptor information and should be included in the list of rejected components.

As a portfolio manager, you validate the components – both existing and proposed – against the component definition. The ones that meet the definition are the qualifying components, as long as they have sufficient key descriptor information. Expert judgment is often used to assess the inputs to the process.

Rejected components and their accompanying information form the second output of the Identification process.

Categorizing components

A pile of mail is just an undeliverable mess until it is sorted into local or international, then by zip code, and also by type of service. Likewise, qualified portfolio components must be sorted or categorized into useful groupings.

Once the Identification process has generated its primary output – the list of qualifying components and associated key descriptor information – this becomes the primary input, along with the organization's strategic plan, to the next process – Categorization.

The Categorization process organizes identified components into meaningful business groups based on the strategic goals they address. Once they are categorized, components within a category can be evaluated, selected, prioritized, and balanced using similar criteria.

Categorizing components allows an organization to balance its investments, or alternately its risks, between all strategic categories and goals.

Once grouped, components can be measured on the same basis, regardless of their origin in the organization. For example, a product research and development (R&D) project can be categorized with all other R&D projects throughout the company, whether they are for other new product ideas or for improvements to the production line.

It could then be measured, compared, evaluated, and prioritized relative to similar components for purposes of the R&D budget.

Categories may include subcategories, such as size, duration, component type, or phase. Subcategories are useful for developing comparative tables, graphs, or charts.

Since the strategic plan of an organization can evolve over time and thus strategic goals may change, categories based on altered goals are subject to change as well.

Categories need to be clearly defined throughout the organization, and are usually relatively limited in number. They may be broadly defined as research and development projects, new product developments, and maintenance. Or more narrow categories are also possible, such as

- profit increase,
- efficiency efforts,
- legal compliance,
- market expansion,
- process improvement,
- business imperatives.

Establishing categories

"The strategic plan for our company calls for improving the quality of our products, maintaining a high standard of customer service, and at least 5% annual business growth. Based on these goals, I have defined three categories for components to be assigned to: quality improvement, customer service, and growth."

Assigning components

"Of the two components that qualified during the Identification process, Component D – the project to develop a more user-friendly manual – clearly fits under customer service. Component A, the high-school-targeted marketing program, is expected to increase revenues by 15%, give a return on investment of 10%, and increase the customer base by 10%. It belongs under the growth category."

Question

Identify the key activities of the Categorization process.

Options:

1. Comparing components to criteria to choose a single category for each component

2. Establishing categories based on the strategic plan

3. Comparing all inventoried components to the component definition

4. Maintaining and adjusting the component mix as needed

Answer

Option 1: This is a correct option. The second activity of the Categorization process is to compare components to the criteria for each category to assign each component to one and only one category.

Option 2: This is a correct option. The first thing that must be done in the Categorization process is to establish categories based on strategic objectives from the strategic plan.

Option 3: This is an incorrect option. Comparing components to the component definition is a main activity of the Identification process, not part of the Categorization process.

Option 4: This is an incorrect option. Maintaining the component mix is not a part of the Categorization process or even the Aligning Process Group.

The Categorization process has a single output – a complete list of components where each and every one has been assigned to a single category.

This categorized list and its associated key descriptor information, become inputs to the Evaluation process that follows. The strategic plan is the other necessary input to the Evaluation process, just as it has been to all processes in the Aligning Process Group so far.

Evaluating components

The Evaluation process involves gathering all pertinent information to evaluate components, and summarizing it to make it possible to compare components meaningfully in the processes that follow.

Qualitative and quantitative data from a variety of sources in the organization is gathered and summarized for each component. The summary data may be presented in graphic form, as documents, or as recommendations. It may be necessary to gather data several times to ensure accuracy.

Question

Identify the inputs to the Evaluation process.

Options:

1. Strategic plan
2. Categorized list of components

3. List of identified components and associated key descriptor information

4. Key descriptor information

5. List of rejected components

Answer

Option 1: This is a correct option. The strategic plan continues to be used throughout the aligning processes to ensure that criteria are based on strategic objectives.

Option 2: This is a correct option. It is the categorized list of components that is a necessary input to evaluation since components must be evaluated within the meaningful business groupings that have been established.

Option 3: This is an incorrect option. The list of identified components is not an acceptable input to the Evaluation process until it has been categorized, thus allowing for comparison within meaningful groups.

Option 4: This is a correct option. The key descriptor information will be used in the Evaluation process to compare components.

Option 5: This is an incorrect option. The list of rejected components is an output of the Identification process but does not form an input to any other alignment process.

Components can be evaluated using a weighted key criteria scoring model. This scoring model uses a series of evaluation criteria, such as strategic alignment, profitability, legal compliance, or risks, and weights their relative importance to the evaluation. Components are scored on each criterion. Totals of the criteria values give an overall rating for the component.

Clearly defined criteria and careful scoring ensure consistent evaluation from component to component.

There are six steps to constructing a weighted scoring model.

Establish the criteria

Establish a list of criteria, grouping them wherever possible. For instance, if criteria 1-4 all reflect some aspect of business profitability – market expansion, increased revenues, ROI, and cost reduction – group these together as indicators of profit.

Description of a weighted key criteria scoring model table follows.

The same weighted key criteria scoring model table with the criteria name column filled in and highlighted.

Description ends.

Decide on weights

Decide on the relative weights of the criteria and express them as percentages.

Description of a weighted key criteria scoring model table follows.

The same weighted key criteria scoring model table with the criteria name column and the weights column filled.

Description ends.

Decide on scoring

Choose a scoring model – for example, a scale of 1-10 or 1-100. If low, medium, and high ratings are more appropriate, use 0, 5, and 10 to represent them.

Score the components

Assign a score for each criterion – based on gathered data – for each component.

Description of a weighted key criteria scoring model table follows.

The same weighted key criteria scoring model table with the criteria name column, the weights column, and the score column filled in.

Description ends.

Calculate criteria score

For each component, multiply the score by the weight to get a total score for each criterion.

Description of a weighted key criteria scoring model table follows.

The same weighted key criteria scoring model table with the criteria name column, the weights column, the score column, and the total column filled in.

Description ends.

Total the scores

Add the criteria totals for each component to get its overall score.

Description of a weighted key criteria scoring model table follows.

The same weighted key criteria scoring model table completed and showing the component total score at the bottom of the total column.

Description ends.

Ed, a portfolio manager for Red Rock Mountain Jeep Tours, has four portfolio components. Two of these are in the maintenance category, and two are in new revenues. He evaluates each of them relative to five criteria he developed from the strategic plan.

Ed: The five criteria are: strategic alignment, customer satisfaction, return on investment (ROI), business risk, and employee satisfaction.

Ed: These criteria are not equal in terms of their relative importance to the strategic plan, so I've weighted them accordingly. My company's conservative approach means that less emphasis is placed on ROI and more on avoiding risk and staying the corporate course.

Ed: The weights break down as follows: strategic alignment – 25%, customer satisfaction – 20%, ROI – 10%, business risk – 35%, and employee satisfaction – 10%.

Ed: After considering all available key descriptor information, I rated each component on a scale from 1-10. I then multiplied the weights by the ratings to generate a final score for each criterion. Totaling the criteria scores gave me an overall score for each component.

After developing five criteria that pertained to the company's strategic objectives, Ed was able to evaluate the components that comprise his maintenance and new revenues categories.

He weighted his criteria relative to their overall importance to this evaluation and then scored them based on the information he gathered. His total scores for each component will allow for valid comparison in subsequent processes.

Generating graphical representations is another key activity of the Evaluation process. This enables simple visual summaries of components' comparative values.

An example of a useful graphic tool is a two-criteria comparison grid. These simple grids are among the most frequently used and effective ways to compare components that must meet more that one criterion. A typical pair of criteria used by organizations might be revenue versus risk.

To use a two-criteria comparison grid you
- choose the two criteria,

- measure and score each project under each criterion,
- construct a grid – a simple graph with x and y axes increasing from left to right and bottom to top respectively,
- position each component in the grid based on its score: for example, those that rank high for both criteria go in the top right.

Regardless of the presentation method, whether passed on as graphics, documents, or as recommendations, the important thing is that the Evaluation process establishes a value for each component that can be meaningfully compared to values of the other components.

The outputs of the Evaluation process are a list of evaluated components with their scores, any useful graphical comparisons and summaries, and any recommendations for the Selection process.

Question

Distinguish between examples of the activities associated with the Categorization and Evaluation processes by matching the processes to appropriate examples. You may use each option more than once.

Options:

A. Categorization process

B. Evaluation process

Targets:

1. Jon ensures that each component is assigned to one grouping

2. Louise scores the components on 10 criteria derived from the company's goals

3. When compared to the criteria, 10 of the components relate to risk reduction and 13 more closely align with revenue growth

4. Ben uses graphical representations to make his recommendations clear

Answer

This is an example of a Categorization process activity. Every component must be assigned to one and only one category.

This is an example of an Evaluation process activity. Criteria are developed based on the strategic goals of the organization and then components are scored on them.

This is an example of a Categorization process activity. Criteria are used to determine which single category a component will fall under.

This is an example of an Evaluation process activity. Summarizing the component scores may be done graphically and, if necessary, recommendations can be made for the Selection process.

Selecting components

After completing the Categorization and Evaluation processes, Ed has a list of categorized and scored components. He is eager to get his projects underway so he begins authorizing the components. He quickly realizes he has neither the funding nor the human resources needed to successfully complete some of the projects.

Knowing how components score in relation to strategic goals is not enough. You still have to consider the organization's capacities before choosing which components to include. And then, you must decide which ones are more important than others.

That's where the Selection and Prioritization processes come into play.

The fourth process of the Aligning Process Group is the Selection process. Using the outputs of the Evaluation process as a starting point, the Selection process goes on to include or exclude the components based on their evaluation scores and other relevant information. This produces an even shorter list of the most desirable components, which can then be prioritized.

The outputs from the prior Evaluation process – the list of categorized and evaluated components, the value scores for each component, and any graphic representations and recommendations – form the primary inputs for selection.

As always, alignment with the organization's strategic plan is required – so it too is an input. Additional information about organizational resources and capabilities also informs the Selection process.

When selection is complete, there are two outputs: a list of categorized, evaluated, and selected components; and any recommendations relevant to prioritizing the components.

Taking the values generated during the Evaluation process, the Selection process compares these against additional information about the organization's ability to meet the proposed components' needs.

Several tools aid in providing this information:

human resource capacity analysis

This shows the organization's ability to handle human resource demands. Performing the analysis by skill set helps identify constraints. Both internal capacity and external resource availability are needed for a complete picture.

financial capacity analysis

This analysis determines the organization's capacity to finance the given components. Both internal finances and external financial availability must be considered.

asset capacity analysis

This analysis is conducted to understand the physical assets that will be required to support the selected components.

The analysis must be done by type of assets – for example, equipment or facilities – to identify the types of constraints generated.

expert judgment

Expert judgment is commonly used to assess technical and management details during many alignment processes.

Here this may include assessing the data gathering methods and the results of the various capacity analyses.

Ed, the portfolio manager for Red Rock Mountain Jeep Tours, is now at the stage where he needs to consider the organization's capacity to execute the proposed components of his portfolio.

Finances

Red Rock Mountain Jeep Tours' finances are adequate to handle all the components in Ed's portfolio.

In addition, the company has a fine balance sheet and an open credit line with its bank of up to $3.5 million, should it be needed.

Assets

The company's equipment is sufficient for all components, and the vehicle inventories were updated just last year.

Ed can see no reason why the company's physical assets would inhibit any of the components of the portfolio.

Human Resources

An analysis of his company's human resources showed that one of the components, a direct marketing campaign to increase revenues, couldn't be handled by the company's current staff.

Since the project was short term, Ed looked outside his company to find a firm that he could hire to handle the marketing. Outsourcing the project proved more expensive than it was projected to be worth, so the project was dropped from the portfolio.

Question

What are the outputs of the Selection process?

Options:

1. List of selected components
2. Recommendations for the Prioritization process
3. List of evaluated components and accompanying key descriptor information
4. Component evaluation scores

Answer

Option 1: This is a correct option. The list of selected components includes components that have been identified, categorized, and evaluated. Then that list is narrowed based on additional organizational capacity data.

Option 2: This is a correct option. In addition to the list of components, any additional recommendations that will further the Prioritization process that follows must be provided.

Option 3: This is an incorrect option. The list of evaluated components is an input to the Selection process, not an output.

Option 4: This is an incorrect option. The evaluation scores are used during the Selection process to help choose the best components. They are not an output of the process, but rather an input.

Prioritizing components

Using established criteria and the outputs of the Selection process – the list of selected components and the recommendations – the Prioritization process follows Selection.

Prioritization ranks components within each strategic or funding category, investment time frame, risk versus return profile, or organizational focus. This ranking supports the subsequent analyses that later are used to balance the portfolio.

The Prioritization process activities include confirming that components are properly categorized. Scores are assigned to components to rank them as to which should receive the highest priority within the portfolio.

The sole output of this process is a list of prioritized components within each strategic category, accompanied by supporting documentation.

Question

What is the purpose of the Prioritization process?

Options:

1. To rank components within categories to support balancing of the portfolio

2. To develop an up-to-date list of all components to be managed as part of the portfolio

3. To organize identified components into meaningful business groups based on strategic goals

4. To choose components based on evaluation scoring and organizational resource information

Answer

Option 1: This is a correct option. The Prioritization process ranks components within strategic categories according to established criteria.

Option 2: This is an incorrect option. This is the stated purpose of the Identification process, not the Prioritization process.

Option 3: This is an incorrect option. This is the purpose of the Categorization process. Prioritization ranks the selected components within the categories.

Option 4: This is an incorrect option. This describes the Selection process. Prioritization is the process after that, where selected components are ranked.

Just as in the Evaluation process, weighted ranking may be used to determine priority. Also, scoring techniques based on either a single criterion or multiple criteria can be used. As always, expert judgment is useful. In this case, it can be used to validate the inputs used for ranking and any other technical details.

The criteria used to prioritize may even be the same ones that were used in previous processes to evaluate and select components. However, during prioritization, the components are examined as part of a whole to ensure the best possible alignment with the strategic plan.

Projects can be ranked using a single criterion prioritization model. This approach involves pairwise comparisons of projects to rank them. It is particularly useful when qualitative judgments between projects have to be made.

Each project is compared to each of the others on a given criterion, and scored and prioritized using the following steps:

assign scores

Construct a table with the components listed vertically and horizontally. Where the project pairs intersect, put a score of 1 in the row of the project that has the greater value and 0 in the row of the lesser component.

total scores

Add the scores for each row to find the overall component scores.

prioritize

The priority of the projects is reflected in descending order of the scores. Assign first priority to the project with the highest row score and lowest priority to the project with the lowest score.

Janine is prioritizing the four components of her portfolio based on one criterion only – profitability.

Assign scores

Janine fills out a single criterion scoring table by comparing the overall profitability of the four components. She considers many profitability indicators: return on investment, risk reduction, net present value, depreciation of assets, and so on. She then decides for example if component A is better than component B. If it is, she scores A as 1 and B as 0.

Total scores

After completing all of the pairwise comparisons, Janine totals the scores for each component by row to arrive at a final score for each component.

Prioritize

The component with the highest score, component B, is the highest priority. The lowest score is the lowest priority.

You can also compare components using a multiple criteria prioritization model.

After setting up a table comparing multiple components over multiple criteria, you go through the following steps:

enter values

Enter the values for each component for each criterion. Since the values will only be compared within the criteria, it doesn't matter if the values are in different units.

rank components for each criterion

Based on the values, rank the components for each criterion.

score the components

For each component, add the rank numbers and divide that total by the number of criteria measured to produce the component's score.

prioritize the components

The priority of the components is reflected in reverse order of the scores. The project with the highest score has the lowest priority, while the project with the lowest score has the highest priority.

Ed is a portfolio manager for Red Rock Mountain Jeep Tours. Previously – during the Selection process – a human resource analysis reduced his portfolio to three components. He is now prioritizing the three remaining components based on three criteria.

Ed: After entering the values for all the criteria, I used those values to rank the three components under each criterion. For example, under the criterion of predicted annual revenue, Project A will generate $5.4 million, Project B will generate $6.1 million, and Project C will generate $2.2 million. They therefore rank as 2, 1, and 3 respectively.

Ed: For the second criterion – cost reduction – the projects ranked 1, 3, and 2 respectively. For strategic alignment, they ranked as 3, 1, and 2.

Ed: Adding the rank amounts across the criteria gives totals of 6, 5, and 7. I divide each of these by 3 – the number of criteria – to get final scores for components. The scores for Projects A, B, and C were 2, 1.67, 2.33 respectively.

Ed: The lowest score has the highest priority. So Project B comes out on top, followed by Project A, and then C.

Ed is a portfolio manager for Red Rock Mountain Jeep Tours. Previously – during the Selection process – a human resource analysis reduced his portfolio to three components. He is now prioritizing the three remaining components based on three criteria.

Ed: After entering the values for all the criteria, I used those values to rank the three components under each criterion. For example, under the criterion of predicted annual revenue, Project A will generate $5.4 million, Project B will generate $6.1 million, and Project C will generate $2.2 million. They therefore rank as 2, 1, and 3 respectively.

Ed: For the second criterion – cost reduction – the projects ranked 1, 3, and 2 respectively. For strategic alignment, they ranked as 3, 1, and 2.

Ed: Adding the rank amounts across the criteria gives totals of 6, 5, and 7. I divide each of these by 3 – the number of criteria – to get final scores for components. The scores for Projects A, B, and C were 2, 1.67, 2.33 respectively.

Ed: The lowest score has the highest priority. So Project B comes out on top, followed by Project A, and then C.

Although Project A excelled at cost reduction, using the multiple criteria model let Ed determine that when all three criteria were taken into account, Project B deserved the highest priority.

Case Study: Question 1 of 3
Scenario

You are a portfolio manager for a manufacturing company. Three projects have been selected for inclusion in your portfolio. You must now prioritize them based on their market expansion predictions, their new revenue predictions, and their potential risk reduction.

Question

Once the measured values have been entered for each component under each criterion, the next step is ranking each of the components within each criterion.

Match the criteria to the correct ranking of components.

Options:

A. Criterion 1– market expansion prediction

B. Criterion 2 – new revenue predictions

C. Criterion 3 – potential risk reduction

215

Targets:

1. Projects A, Project B, and Project C rank as 1, 3, 2
2. Projects A, Project B, and Project C rank as 3, 2, 1
3. Projects A, Project B, and Project C rank as 2, 3, 1

Answer

The respective values for the market expansion prediction criterion are 10%, 3%, and 5%. This results in a ranking of 1, 3, and 2.

The potential risk reduction values of 4%, 6%, and 7% cause the three projects to rank as 3, 2, and 1 respectively.

The values for new revenue predictions – 3.2, 1.2, and 5.1 – result in a respective ranking of 2, 3, and 1.

Case Study: Question 2 of 3

Calculating overall component scores is the next step in the multiple criteria scoring comparison. Recall that Project A ranked first, second, and third for the various criteria. Project B ranked third, third, and second and Project C ranked second, first, and first.

Match the component projects to the appropriate scores.

Options:

A. Project A
B. Project B
C. Project C

Targets:

1. 2
2. 2.67
3. 1.33

Answer

Adding the individual rankings for Project A – 1, 2, and 3 – gives a total of 6. That figure is then divided by 3 – the number of criteria – to arrive at a score of 2.

Adding the individual rankings for Project B gives a total of 8. That figure is then divided by the number of criteria to arrive at the score of 2.67.

The rankings for Project C add up to a total of 4. That figure is then divided by 3, which is the number of criteria, to arrive at the score of 1.33.

Case Study: Question 3 of 3

Based on the final scores you calculated for each component – Project A scored 2, Project B scored 2.67, and Project C scored 1.33 – which statements reflect the correct prioritization and reasoning?

Options:

1. Project C has the highest priority, as it has the lowest overall score
2. Project C has the highest priority, as it has the highest overall score
3. Project B has the lowest priority, as it has the highest overall score
4. Project A has the lowest priority, as it has the lowest overall score

Answer

Option 1: This is a correct option. The priority of the components is reflected in the reverse order of the scores. Project C has the lowest score and therefore gets the highest priority.

Option 2: This is an incorrect option. Actually, Project C has the lowest score and that's why it has the highest priority. The scores and priorities have an inverse relationship.

Option 3: This is a correct option. Since the priority of the components is reflected in reverse order of the scores, Project B's highest score makes it the lowest priority.

Option 4: This is an incorrect option. Project A is assigned the middle priority since it has neither the high nor the low score.

To successfully prioritize the three projects in the previous scenario, you need to know how to set up a table and complete a multiple criteria scoring model.

You rank each project for each of the three criteria, total the component rankings by row, and then divide by three – the number of criteria – to get an overall score for each component project.

Then, remembering that priorities are inversely related to the scores, you assign the highest priority to Project C and the lowest to Project B.

Balancing components

Anna, a portfolio manager, thinks her portfolio has too many short-term projects. Most of these will have very little impact on increasing market share, her company's current mission. She could use more long- term visionary projects that might lead to major market breakthroughs.

She also thinks the allocations for maintenance are disproportionately large. The maintenance budget belongs to a group of veteran managers whose long standing at the company seems to give their departments preferential treatment around budget time.

These are issues of portfolio imbalance.

The Portfolio Balancing process determines the portfolio component mix that will best support the organization's strategic initiatives and achieve strategic goals. Portfolio balancing ensures that resource planning and resource allocation are tied to company strategy.

219

And portfolio balancing maximizes portfolio return, while taking into account the organization's predefined acceptable level of risk. Like an investment portfolio, business portfolios need to balance risk and reward and optimally diversify.

There are five inputs to the Portfolio Balancing process:

list of prioritized components organized by strategic category

The sole output from the Prioritization process is this list of prioritized components and associated supporting documentation, which becomes the starting point for portfolio balancing.

portfolio management criteria

At the portfolio level, portfolio managers must often meet certain defined objectives and adhere to guidelines regarding investment diversification, acceptable risk, and expected financial return.

portfolio performance metrics

Metrics are established by the organization as to portfolio return, risk, diversification, and so on. These metrics indicate whether the portfolio is performing as expected or whether it needs adjustment.

capacity constraints

The capacity constraints are the limitations caused by the organization's financial, physical, and human resource assets.

portfolio rebalancing recommendations

From time to time, as the portfolio is reviewed, recommendations may be made to terminate or realign existing components. Portfolio balancing is used to validate that any changes to the portfolio enhance the portfolio's ability to accomplish strategic goals.

Shannon is an experienced portfolio manager at Sonical Electronics, a manufacturer of entertainment hardware. She is balancing her regional portfolio.

Components and their capacities

"The list of prioritized components generated by the Prioritization process showed my five qualified projects and two programs in descending order of importance. An analysis showed that Projects A and B were most advantageous. Both required significant resources.

Using a scenario analysis, I compared two possible mixes: one where Project A received 40% of the development budget while B received 20%, and then one where A received 50% and B received 30%. The higher percentages of the budget were predicted to work better."

Portfolio criteria and metrics

"At the portfolio level, portfolio managers are required to keep overseas outsourcing to less than 30% of the budget, while showing a 20% rate of return on investment to support the company's growth initiative.

Since Project B will represent 30% of the budget, I outsourced that one and kept all others in- house."

Balancing the portfolio involves reviewing selected and prioritized portfolio components, and optimizing the component mix. Based on predefined portfolio management criteria, such as desired risk profile, portfolio performance metrics, and capacity constraints, the component mix is adjusted to support the organization's strategic objectives.

The balancing process also considers relationships, interdependencies, and synergies that exist between components. It analyzes whether enhancing these interconnections generates a greater return or cost savings.

An automobile manufacturer found that the ever-increasing number of microprocessors used in modern vehicles – as many as 50 or more per vehicle – meant that two of the projects in a certain portfolio had related needs.

Similar requirements

The ongoing project for developing a more fuel-efficient engine and the new project for creating an onboard GPS system both required the use of the same kind of electronics testing equipment.

Savings

Rather than establishing separate labs for each project – with the corresponding separate staffs, budgets, paperwork, and so on – a decision was made to expand and upgrade the equipment in the current manufacturing testing lab.

Allocating resources to this upgrade allows the current lab to accommodate the volume of testing required by both projects.

Question

What are the inputs to the Portfolio Balancing process?

Options:

1. A list of prioritized components organized by strategic category
2. Portfolio management criteria
3. Portfolio performance metrics
4. Capacity constraints
5. Any portfolio rebalancing recommendations
6. The list of categorized components
7. Component evaluation scores

Answer

Option 1: This is a correct option. The list of prioritized components organized by strategic category – the sole output from the Prioritization process – is the basis for portfolio balancing.

Option 2: This is a correct option. Criteria that the organization has established at the portfolio level must be considered when balancing.

Option 3: This is a correct option. Metrics regarding performance of the portfolio as a whole must be considered when balancing components.

Option 4: This is a correct option. Portfolio-level constraints are an input since they must be considered during balancing.

Option 5: This is a correct option. As portfolios are reviewed over time, suggestions for rebalancing are made and these must be considered as an input.

Option 6: This is an incorrect option. The component list that forms an input to portfolio balancing must be selected and prioritized, as well as categorized.

Option 7: This is an incorrect option. The evaluation scores have already served their purpose during the Selection process. They are not a useful input for balancing the component mix.

During the Portfolio Balancing process there are several tools available:

quantitative analysis

Quantitative analysis may include the use of spreadsheets or other tools to examine factors of interest such as cash flow.

cost benefit analysis

Balancing may be based on any organizationally preferred financial analysis method, for example Net

Present Value (NPV), Internal Rate of Return (IRR), or cost benefit ratio.

scenario analysis

Scenario analysis is a sort of "What if...?" analysis that may involve the use of multiple baselines. It is used to balance the portfolio by considering different combinations of current and potential components.

probability analysis

Probability analyses that employ decision trees, flowcharts, or computer-based systems simulations are used to compare components based on success and failure probabilities for desired criteria, such as estimated cost, anticipated revenues, or potential risk.

expert judgment

Expert judgment is often used to assess the inputs needed for balancing the portfolio.

graphical analytical models

Graphical methods – such as risk-return charts, histograms, pie charts, and bubble diagrams – are used to evaluate the portfolio mix.

One of the most commonly used types of graphical models is the bubble diagram. These diagrams compare the component mix to pre-established "balancing and monitoring" criteria. Each bubble represents a project, with size and color available to represent additional variables such as cost or net present value.

Keep in mind that graphical models are for information display. They are not decision models per se – as they don't provide the neat numerical ranking of, for example, the decision models used in prioritization.

Balancing activities determine whether to maintain the status quo or adjust the portfolio.

There are three outputs of the balancing process:

- a list of approved portfolio components ready for execution as planned, or after developing a business case to confirm their feasibility,
- updated master list of approved, inactivated, and terminated elements and the rationales for any that were removed,
- updated approved portfolio component allocations.

How do you know whether the right balance is there in the first place? Even veteran portfolio managers have trouble defining the right balance of projects. Basically, a good portfolio mix is one in which the set of components is balanced in terms of the key parameters that are being applied.

It can be difficult to determine balance unless a portfolio is noticeably out of balance. While there are some rules of thumb about the best splits in long-term versus short-term projects, high-risk versus low- risk, and so on, unlike the outputs from evaluation and prioritization, the result is not a convenient rank- ordered list of preferred projects.

Shannon, a portfolio manager for Sonical Electronics, has balanced her regional portfolio.

Shannon: My list of approved components totals seven – five projects and two programs. They are all ready to go as originally planned except for the budget changes.

Shannon: Since no components were deactivated or terminated as a result of balancing the portfolio, the master list will be essentially the same as the list of approved components.

Shannon: The balancing changes to the portfolio mean that 60% of the portfolio budget will have to be allocated to Project A and 30% to Project B.

Question

What are the outputs of the Portfolio Balancing process?

Options:

1. A list of approved portfolio components ready for execution as planned

2. Updated master list of approved, inactivated, and terminated elements and rationale for removal

3. Updated approved portfolio components' allocations

4. A list of prioritized components by strategic category

5. Revised portfolio-level criteria

Answer

Option 1: This is a correct option. The approved component list becomes the basis, along with the approved budget and resource allocations, for the Authorization process that follows.

Option 2: This is a correct option. The Portfolio Balancing process generates a list that includes approved components, and also those that have been removed after consideration of the portfolio mix and the portfolio-level criteria. Rationale for excluding the components must accompany this output.

Option 3: This is a correct option. Portfolio balancing outputs as to budget and resource allocations must be sent to the final aligning process to be authorized and then communicated to the organization as a whole.

Option 4: This is an incorrect option. The list of prioritized components is an input, not an output of the Portfolio Balancing process.

Option 5: This is an incorrect option. Although portfolio-level criteria may need to be adjusted from time to time, this is not an output of the Portfolio Balancing process but rather a strategic planning issue.

Authorizing components

Once the portfolio has been balanced and the decisions have been made, it's time to make things happen. That's the job of the Authorization process.

The Authorization process is an action step that formally authorizes funds for developing the selected components. It also involves communicating the portfolio balancing decisions.

The Authorization process relies on several inputs:
- the list of approved portfolio components,
- budget requirements for components,
- resource requirements for components,
- the list of inactivated or terminated components.

The key activities of this process include authorizing and allocating the budgets and resources for selected components – including reallocating budgets and resources freed up by inactivated or terminated components.

Authorization involves effectively communicating to key stakeholders both the balancing decisions made regarding the components included in the portfolio and the status of excluded components. It also involves assigning roles, responsibilities, and performance milestones and expectations – such as timetables and metrics – for implementation and monitoring.

Question

What are the inputs to the Authorization process?

Options:

1. A list of approved portfolio components
2. Component budget requirements
3. Component resource requirements
4. A list of inactivated or terminated components
5. The strategic plan
6. Component scores

Answer

Option 1: This is a correct option. The list of approved portfolio components is the basis for the Authorization process.

Option 2: This is a correct option. For components to get underway, component budget requirements must be presented so they can be authorized.

Option 3: This is a correct option. Resource requirements for components must be provided so they can be authorized.

Option 4: This is a correct option. A list of inactivated or terminated components is vital to reallocating their budget and resource requirements – all of which must be communicated to the organization.

Option 5: This is an incorrect option. At this point in the processes of the Aligning Process Group, the strategic plan has played its part and does not itself form an input into the Authorization process.

Option 6: This is an incorrect option. Component scores were useful in earlier processes. But now that the components have been selected, prioritized, and balanced, scores do not play a part.

The Authorization process activities rely on tools, such as portfolio management roles and responsibilities documents, which identify stakeholders, define roles, and specify responsibilities for all participants in the portfolio management process.

Another tool is the portfolio management communication plan, which defines all communication needs, identifies recipients, and sets out communication requirements including frequency of communication.

The Authorization process has six outputs:

- additions to the active component inventory,
- updated performance expectations,
- approved component budgets and exceptions,
- approved component resource allocations and exceptions,
- list of excluded components,
- portfolio milestones.

To complete the Authorization process, Shannon, a portfolio manager working for Sonical Electronics, formally allocated resources by signing off on the finished budgets for her seven components.

At the portfolio managers' meeting, she presented her updated performance expectations and milestone dates for her portfolio. Her presentation showed that two of the included components were additions to the active component inventory, and no components were excluded as a result of balancing.

Shannon's final documentation informed management in general – and the affected project managers in particular – of the decision made during portfolio balancing to increase the percentages of the budget assigned to Projects A and B.

Question

What are the outputs of the Authorization process?

Options:

1. Additions to the active component inventory

2. Updated performance expectations

3. Approved component budgets and exceptions

4. Approved component resource allocations and exceptions

5. Excluded components

6. Portfolio milestones

7. Component definitions

8. Capacity analyses

Answer

Option 1: This is a correct option. Although many of the components in a given portfolio may already be active, any newly added components must be included in the inventory.

Option 2: This is a correct option. Any changes to expectations of the portfolio or its components that arise during aligning processes must be communicated as an output of authorization.

Option 3: This is a correct option. The budget decisions reached must be formally authorized so that projects may begin.

Option 4: This is a correct option. Resource allocations must be formally authorized and communicated much the same way that budget allocations are, and so form an output of authorization.

Option 5: This is a correct option. The components to be excluded are decisions of the balancing process that must be communicated at authorization so that these components can be re-evaluated and reassigned as needed.

Option 6: This is a correct option. Milestones at the portfolio level must be communicated to the rest of the organization during the Authorization process.

Option 7: This is an incorrect option. Component definitions were used in the Identification process to qualify components for consideration. They are not an output of authorization.

Option 8: This is an incorrect option. Capacity analyses are not an output of authorization, they are tools used during portfolio balancing.

Section 2 - The Monitoring and Controlling Process Group

Section 2 - The Monitoring and Controlling Process Group

The Portfolio Reporting and Reviewing process and the Strategic Change process make up the Monitoring and Controlling Process Group. These two processes work to ensure that portfolio management can adjust for the effects of the environment, including changes to the basic organizational strategy. They verify that the reality of the portfolio activities matches up with the intention behind using the Aligning Process Group – an optimized and strategically aligned portfolio.

This lesson will explain the basic activities, tools, inputs, and outputs associated with the Monitoring and Controlling Process Group.

The Portfolio Reporting and Review process is portfolio management's watchdog. Its activities revolve around ensuring that portfolio components remain aligned with strategic initiatives and that resources are appropriately assigned and used.

Once the Aligning Process Group has set the course of action for the portfolio and work has begun, the

Monitoring and Controlling Process Group's Portfolio Reporting and Review process ensures continued alignment and optimization.

The Strategic Change process uses the data from the Portfolio Reporting and Review process to anticipate and adjust for fundamental changes to the strategic direction.

By using two inputs – the portfolio reporting and review data and any strategic plan updates – this process helps adjust the criteria used to align and review portfolio components.

Overview of monitoring and controlling

Things change. It is a fact of life and most certainly a fact of project and portfolio management.

In turbulent times, Abraham Lincoln once said "The dogmas of the quiet past are inadequate to the stormy present." When dealing with portfolio management, the best laid management plans can become "dogmas of the past" unless they are monitored and occasionally re-evaluated.

The Aligning Process Group ensures that portfolio management considers strategic alignment throughout the various aligning processes. But after project authorization, the business environment begins to have its effect. As projects and programs get underway, scope may start to creep, budgets may be exceeded, or milestones missed.

Even positive changes – such as greater than expected returns or coming in under budget – can have effects on the portfolio that require adjustments to be made for optimum performance. Larger adjustments may be needed if major changes come at a strategic level.

The Monitoring and Controlling Process Group reviews performance indicators to assure continued alignment with organizational strategy and the most effective use of resources.

The kinds of variations that you may have observed in your own projects are precisely the changes the Monitoring and Controlling Process Group deals with across a portfolio.

The Monitoring and Controlling Process Group is responsible for two processes:

• the Portfolio Reporting and Review process,
• the Strategic Change process.

The Portfolio Reporting and Review process involves gathering and reporting on performance indicators, periodically re-examining the portfolio. Using this process verifies that the portfolio contains only the components that best support the achievement of the strategic goals and that resources are used effectively.

Feedback from various projects and programs is used for monitoring. Information about progress against the portfolio plan, financial results, performance against competitors, customer satisfaction, resource usage, budget usage, and many other factors, is used.

The review process also involves considering performance at the portfolio level, based on characteristics such as portfolio management criteria, dependencies, risk, and financial performance.

It's important to understand the Monitoring and Controlling Process Group because you'll be able to

respond to changes in strategy

The Strategic Change process tracks and integrates changes so portfolio management can respond. The organization can address new business conditions, measure their effect, and take action.

ensure that resources are used effectively

The Portfolio Reporting and Review process involves periodically monitoring resource usage. This ensures that, as the environment changes, the portfolio mix continues to make the best use of resources.

ensure that performance expectations are met

By monitoring characteristics such as performance against the plan, financial performance, and scope creep, the Portfolio Reporting and Review process ensures that delays or poorer returns are adjusted for in time to keep performance on track. Re-evaluating the criteria and metrics used for tracking is also part of the process.

The Portfolio Reporting and Review process can provide direction to project or program managers or component rebalancing recommendations to portfolio management.

It can also make upward recommendations to organizational management as to needed changes in the strategic plan, to the component selection criteria or metrics, or to the portfolio review process itself.

The other process of the Monitoring and Controlling Process Group is the Strategic Change process, which enables portfolio management to respond to changes in strategy.

Small changes to strategy may not require changes to the portfolio. But significant changes may impact the portfolio because the strategic plan is the basis for all alignment processes – such as identification, categorization, and prioritization. Larger strategic changes may result from new leadership wanting to adjust organizational strategy according to different goals, or from market variations that require changes in profit thresholds.

As the environment changes – internally or externally – the organization may also decide to change the criteria used to determine the composition and direction of the portfolio.

The New Product portfolio for a natural foods company benefited greatly from the review of key performance indicators associated with the processes of the Monitoring and Controlling Process Group.

Portfolio Reporting and Review process

The tools used in the Portfolio Reporting and Review process indicated that certain portfolio components weren't performing as expected. Although the portfolio as a whole was performing well, the Schedule Performance Index (SPI) for both the USDA Compliance program and the New-products Training program indicated both were severely out of line with projections.

Since budget-usage indicators showed the Product Development program was running 30% under budget, those funds were reallocated to the delinquent projects to get them back on schedule. The portfolio was rebalanced for a more effective use of resources.

Strategic Change process

The Strategic Change process recently came into play when the company was acquired by a larger corporation. The new parent corporation has a much greater emphasis on controlling risk.

Using the tools of the Strategic Change process, the strategic plan was altered slightly to better align with the new direction. This resulted in revised component definitions and three new measurements for risk assessment being added to the component Evaluation process. A basic change in strategy was quickly and appropriately incorporated.

Question

Why is understanding the Monitoring and Controlling Process Group important?

Options:

1. You will be able to respond to changes in strategy quickly and appropriately

2. You will be able to ensure that resources are used effectively

3. You will be able to start with the portfolio component mix that best supports the organization's strategic goals

4. You will be able to monitor performance and prevent strategic change from occurring

5. You will be able to ensure that performance expectations are met

Answer

Option 1: This is a correct option. The Strategic Change process tracks and takes into account strategic changes to enable portfolio management to respond appropriately.

Option 2: This is a correct option. Even carefully aligned portfolio components typically require adjustment once work begins. For example, environmental factors such as changes in markets can affect predicted component returns and results.

Option 3: This is an incorrect option. The Aligning Process Group works to design the initial component mix. The Monitoring and Controlling Process Group comes into play after work has already begun to ensure continued alignment and optimization.

Option 4: This is an incorrect option. The Monitoring and Controlling Process Group does not prevent strategic change from happening, but rather allows strategic change to occur and enables portfolio management to respond appropriately.

Option 5: This is a correct option. By carefully monitoring actual component performance from a variety of perspectives, adjustments can be made to components, to the portfolio mix, or to the metrics used to measure performance – ensuring goals are met.

Reporting and reviewing

A ship will never arrive at its destination if it is simply launched in the proper direction. Without someone monitoring and correcting its progress, even a well-built ship will drift off course.

Launching a portfolio of projects and programs without a systematic means of monitoring and adjusting progress is a sure way to miss the target once predictions, plans, and theories meet real-world conditions.

The purposes of the Portfolio Reporting and Review process are to ensure that the portfolio contains only components that actually support achievement of the strategic goals – and to make sure that the portfolio makes the best use of resources.

This is accomplished by gathering performance indicators, reporting on them, and reviewing the portfolio at useful intervals to ensure both alignment with organizational strategy and effective resource utilization. For example, you check to see that component projects are on time, on course, and on budget; and that the quality of work is adequate.

The Portfolio Reporting and Review process requires several inputs for its examination of the many aspects of the portfolio. These inputs are

component data

The reviewing and reporting activities rely on the component data gathered throughout the component life cycle – information about progress against plan, budget, actual return, and many other factors.

key performance indicators (KPIs)

KPIs are the metrics used for examining component progress to decide if the results are in line with expectations.

In a call center, a customer service representative would be expected to close a certain number of customer calls. A KPI in this call center environment could be the percentage of issues solved per day.

organizational governance standards, controls, and constraints

Reviewing and reporting activities must take into account organizational governance standards, controls, and constraints as they apply to the portfolio.

Governance standards include human resource and strategic policies. Organizational controls are checkpoints in the normal course of business activities, such as budget processes. Constraints may include the organization's structure. Portfolio managers may be able to exert some influence upon these factors.

environmental constraints

Government regulations, interest rates, and seasonal weather are all examples of environmental constraints. Portfolio managers have no control over these external factors.

Other inputs to the process include

strategic goals and strategy

Components must continue to be aligned with the organization's strategic goals and strategy to qualify for inclusion, receive access to resources, and get funding. Any changes in strategy require at least a minimal review – and major changes, such as a reorganization, may require reassessment of the alignment criteria.

portfolio management criteria

The portfolio management criteria may involve specific objectives, constraints, and guidelines for managing the portfolio. For example, investment diversification objectives and risk tolerance thresholds may be set for the portfolio as a whole.

resource allocation and capacity data

In terms of resource allocation and capacity data, financial, human resources, production allocation, and capacity data are needed for making prioritization and allocation decisions.

evaluation and selection criteria

Portfolio reviews use the evaluation and selection criteria to decide whether to replace a component with some other that will increase the likelihood of achieving strategic goals.

Question

What purposes does the Portfolio Reporting and Review process serve?

Options:

1. It ensures that only components that support achievement of the strategic goals are included

2. It ensures that the portfolio makes the best use of resources

3. It ensures management buy-in to the portfolio management process

4. It ensures that the criteria used to originally align the portfolio continue to be the ones by which it is evaluated and prioritized

Answer

Option 1: This is a correct option. Ensuring that previously aligned components continue to be aligned after work has begun is one of the purposes of reporting and review.

Option 2: This is a correct option. Optimizing the performance of components is another way in which the Portfolio Reporting and Review process increases the likelihood of strategic goal achievement.

Option 3: This is an incorrect option. While the results of the reviewing process may convince reluctant senior management of the need for good portfolio management, that is not its purpose.

Option 4: This is an incorrect option. The Portfolio Reporting and Review process may help portfolio managers come to the conclusion that the original criteria were incorrect.

The outputs of the reporting and reviewing process include recommendations at the portfolio level, as well as directives that flow downward and upward.

Recommendations to component management regarding continuation, realignment of priorities or dependencies, resource reallocation, suspension, or termination of components flow downward.

Reviews may generate portfolio rebalancing recommendations. Funding of particular components may need to be discontinued or components may need realignment to ensure that the component mix still supports strategic objectives and remains on track to achieve stated goals. These recommendations become inputs to the Strategic Change process so that it can determine if the rebalancing changes are sufficient or whether a change to strategy is needed.

The Portfolio Reporting and Review process can also generate upward-flowing recommendations to organizational management. Insights gained during review may lead to recommendations to alter the strategic plan, change component selection criteria, or even revise the portfolio review process itself.

Another output of portfolio reviews is reporting on strategic goal achievement. This is performed periodically, or as needed, to ensure the portfolio's progress is on track.

Other outputs of the Portfolio Reporting and Review process include refined selection criteria, and updated key performance indicators (KPIs).

The criteria used for selection, evaluation, and prioritization may change as an organization evolves. Also, as work gets underway and results start pouring in, the effectiveness of criteria can be evaluated. Portfolio reviews can determine whether using the given criteria actually leads to achievement of the strategic goals or if the criteria should be refined or replaced.

Key performance indicators are used for decision making. KPIs must be re-evaluated to determine if results are being properly driven by the current metrics, and refined as appropriate.

Portfolio Reporting and Review process activities are aimed at ensuring that the portfolio contains only the best components for achieving strategic goals, and that these components are performing in the most efficient and effective manner. These activities include

reviewing component relationships, performance, and predicted performance against portfolio management criteria

Reviewing component relationships, performance, and predicted performance against portfolio management criteria involves rechecking components as to priorities, dependencies, scope, expected returns, risks, and financial performance in light of portfolio control and investment criteria.

reviewing expected impact of business forecasts, resource usage, and capacity constraints on portfolio performance

Reviewing expected impact of business forecasts, resource usage, and capacity constraints on portfolio performance involves keeping an eye on the latest business climate predictions and also the changing availability of resources and other capacities of the business.

reviewing sponsorship accountability and other ownership criteria

Reviewing sponsorship accountability and other ownership criteria involves reviewing how the project or program is reacting to a sponsor and whether communication and project sponsor activities are being properly performed.

identifying components that are not authorized

From time to time, the review process identifies components that are not authorized. As a result of changes incurred after work has begun, components may no longer meet the component definitions that originally qualified them for inclusion in the portfolio.

As a result of the examination of the portfolio, its components, its performance, and the current and expected environmental conditions it faces, other activities must be performed. These include

determining actions to take for components that are no longer aligned

The review process determines the actions to take for components that are no longer aligned. Decisions must then be made whether to continue with, add to, or terminate specific components, or to reprioritize and realign the components with strategic goals.

proposing portfolio management changes

The review process may generate proposed portfolio management changes. Portfolio management may be informed of changes that need to be made to the portfolio management process itself, such as revised selection criteria, increased frequency of review, or better communication policies.

providing direction to component management

Periodic reviews may result in providing direction to component management if changes that should be made at the component level are revealed. Recommendations would then be made downward from portfolio management to project or program management, for example.

Shannon is a portfolio manager for Sonical Electronics, an entertainment hardware manufacturing company. She is reviewing her electronic mobile entertainment portfolio, which has been active for six months.

Reviewing against portfolio criteria

During her review, Shannon's re-examination of components in light of Sonical's portfolio control and investment criteria indicates that the portfolio as a whole is not measuring up to the organizational requirement of keeping at least 25% of manufacturing operations US based.

Examining factors impacting portfolio performance

Due to a recent six-month slump in financial indicators, such as the Dow and NASDAQ indices, investor confidence is low and budget cutbacks have been initiated across the board. In addition, consumers are cutting back on spending on entertainment products. Adjustments to the portfolio must be made to ensure all projects come in under their original budgets.

Identifying unauthorized components

If sales continue to decline below expected levels, Project A – the development of a new handheld media player – will have to be terminated. It will no longer meet the component definition requirements.

Reviewing sponsorship, accountability, and ownership

Part of portfolio management's job is to monitor the performance of sponsors as part of the review process and inform executive management of any shortcomings. All sponsors were found to be performing adequately in this review, so no action was required.

As Shannon's review process continues, performance data and market predictions result in adjustment to the portfolio and its components.

Shannon: Market research and projections point to a coming global decline in the popularity of handheld PDAs. I communicated this information to project managers, advising them to alter their budgets and reallocate the resources in anticipation of a 10% drop in sales next year.

Shannon: The portfolio's overall return on investment was in line with original targets for the first six months. However, while going through the data I noticed that during the third and fourth months, there was a seasonal variation in sales. Adjusting for those kinds of seasonal changes could help optimize the portfolio, so I proposed to senior management that the portfolio review schedule should be changed to once every three months.

Shannon: Part of the review process is determining what to do about misaligned components. Return on investment and earned value statistics show that Project B is not living up to expectations and has fallen below the requirement of the component definition to generate at least a 10% sales increase. Adding additional resources could help. This component will have to be reprioritized and realigned.

Shannon's Portfolio Reporting and Review process examined many aspects of the portfolio.

Factors affecting the portfolio or its components, such as a financial downturn and a poor market projection, led to downward-flowing directives to component management.

The portfolio management process itself had to be adjusted to increase the frequency of reviews, so that recommendation was made upward to organizational management.

Reviewing the portfolio and its components against the criteria they are subject to indicated shortfalls in the portfolio as a whole, and in a particular project that required realignment.

The tools and techniques associated with reporting and review are primarily concerned with monitoring portfolios for continued balance and alignment, and ensuring components perform as expected. They include the

project portfolio management system

The project portfolio management system is typically a central electronic repository where component-level information is stored, so it can be accessed and summarized by portfolio management for analysis and decision making. This repository is usually integrated with the systems and applications used by the individual component projects and programs.

financial reporting system

The financial reporting system, another important tool, also provides information upon which portfolio managers base their decisions. Whether portfolio management is performed by a single person or a team, information provided by these financial systems is used to decide whether to remove, reprioritize, or realign components.

performance measurement techniques

The performance measurement techniques at the portfolio level measure progress much the same way as component progress is measured, with indicators such as earned value. The value resulting from the component's progress – its contribution to strategic goals – is determined using performance indicators and models that measure strategic performance.

Case Study: Question 1 of 3

Scenario

Ed is a portfolio manager for Red Rock Mountain Jeep Tours. His portfolio has been active for a year and it is time to carry out his review.

Answer the questions in order.

Question

Ed is new to the Portfolio Reporting and Review process. Identify the activities he should engage in first.

Options:

1. Three of the tour programs use the same equipment. Ed checks Project A and it fails to stay within usage limits as defined in the Performance Management Plan.

2. He reviews the company's human resource policy, which limits overtime, in order to determine the amount of work hours that could be applied to projects.

3. He considers business forecasts for the tour market and waits to see if they are right.

4. He reduced resources for the customer satisfaction program, as it no longer meets the component definition.

Answer

Option 1: This is a correct option. Reporting and reviewing activities include rechecking priorities and dependencies in light of portfolio control criteria.

Option 2: This is a correct option. Portfolio reviews must take into account organizational constraints such as human resource policies.

Option 3: This is an incorrect option. Part of the Portfolio Reporting and Review process is taking business forecasts into account rather than simply waiting to see what will happen.

Option 4: This is an incorrect option. Reallocating resources is certainly an appropriate balancing activity, but components that no longer meet the component definition should be realigned or removed rather than reduced and left to linger.

Case Study: Question 2 of 3

Select further suitable activities for Ed to complete during the Portfolio Reporting and Review process.

Options:

1. The executive sponsor for the Internet promotion project is doing a poor job of securing needed resources for the project manager. Ed documents this and organizational management is informed.

2. When Project A falls behind, Ed works weekends with the project manager to ensure timely product delivery.

3. Ed automatically terminates components that no longer meet the component definition.

4. Based on a KPI – customer satisfaction rating - he decides to realign two projects that have ratings below what's allowed by the component definition.

Answer

Option 1: This is a correct option. Sponsorship and ownership responsibilities are reviewed and reported on by portfolio management.

Option 2: This is an incorrect option. Project managers are responsible for getting their work done. Portfolio managers must take a higher view and see that the right work gets done.

Option 3: This is an incorrect option. Portfolio management must make decisions as to whether to terminate, continue with, or reprioritize and realign components with corporate strategy.

Option 4: This is a correct option. One of the primary activities of the review process is to use KPIs to identify components that no longer qualify for inclusion in the portfolio and take appropriate action.

Case Study: Question 3 of 3

Identify the other reporting and review activities Ed must complete.

Options:

1. Ed recommends that the executives change the review frequency from yearly to monthly, as several chances to optimize the portfolio were missed.

2. Ed removes the package sales project because it isn't producing the predicted ROI. Based on the KPIs, it no longer meets the component definition.

3. The KPIs showed that Project C isn't performing well due to incorrect selection criteria. Ed directs the component manager to fix the issue.

4. Data shows that project schedules are too tight, causing too much rework. Ed directs the component manager to relax project milestones.

5. Two of the projects no longer meet the component definition, but are performing well so Ed alters the definition to allow them to remain in the portfolio.

Answer

Option 1: This is a correct option. Portfolio managers may find itself making upward recommendations to the executive level regarding the portfolio management process itself and how to improve it.

Option 2: This is a correct option. The review process generates decisions whether to continue with, add to, or terminate specific components; or whether to just reprioritize and realign them with strategic goals.

Option 3: Incorrect. While the review process may determine that the portfolio is being adversely affected by incorrect selection criteria, project managers are not equipped or authorized to fix portfolio alignment.

Option 4: This is a correct option. Downward-flowing recommendations to component management represent a common type of portfolio reporting and review activity.

Option 5: Incorrect. The component definition is carefully aligned with strategic goals. Components that don't meet the definition are no longer authorized and may be terminated, suspended, or revised to align.

Dealing with strategic change

At Alan's company, most of the upper-level managers who supported the Six Sigma quality initiative have left the firm. The newer managers are much more interested in focusing on Just-in-Time (JIT) delivery strategies but, as yet, no formal revision has been made to the strategic plan. The various projects and programs are competing for resources and seem to be heading in two different directions.

When supportive leaders and managers are replaced by people who are uninterested in – or even opposed to – an existing strategy, updates to the strategic plan may occur. Criteria may then need to be revised in order to select projects that better align with the current corporate goals.

The second and final process of the Monitoring and Controlling Process Group is the Strategic Change process. It exists to enable portfolio management to respond to changes in strategy.

Although small changes may not affect the management process sufficiently to trigger the strategic change process, larger changes may require revision of the strategic plan or selection criteria – resulting in the reprioritization of components and rebalancing of portfolios.

The Strategic Change process works with just two inputs:

portfolio reporting and review

The Portfolio Reporting and Review process periodically examines and reports on portfolio and component performance and achievement of organizational goals.

This process may produce recommendations to organizational management to alter the strategic plan. When a major change such as this occurs, the criteria used for component alignment must be reassessed as well.

strategic plan updates

Strategic plan updates may be needed to reflect changes in the mission, to organizational priorities, or to long-term objectives and the planned means of achieving them.

The Strategic Change process works to anticipate and adapt to these changes.

The Strategic Change process uses various tools and techniques for tracking and taking into account strategic changes. Three tools that help the organization effectively consider new business conditions that arise are

expert judgment

criteria re-weighting graphical representations

As in almost any process, expert judgment can be used to assess any technical and management details. In the Strategic Change process, experts are frequently used to decide if a strategic change will occur and what its effect on the portfolio will be. Such experts might include technical specialists assigned to the project, external professional associations, or government bodies.

Strategic changes may require re-weighting the criteria used to align the original portfolio components. Revising, re-weighting, or developing new criteria for realignment of the components in a portfolio can address new business conditions.

Graphics can be used to represent data and relationships. Such representations can clarify needed criteria changes by indicating overlapping areas of responsibility, changes in criteria importance over time, or divergent objectives.

All three tools are aimed at helping to measure the effect of new business conditions on current strategy in order to determine what to do. The tools are

expert judgment

At a ceramics manufacturing company, experts from an HR association were hired to examine the HR process. They suggested the creation of an employee interaction program, a new program designed to respond to the low morale problem associated with the recent takeover. This new component was included in the HR portfolio.

criteria re-weighting

A national chain of music stores geared most of its strategies toward outcompeting its only significant competitor. When that other giant corporation suddenly folded, the chain lost its primary opponent. Dramatic changes to existing strategies were required to enable the company to secure the market before other competition stepped in. Component selection criteria were altered to reflect the changing face of the business landscape.

graphical representations

After last year's merger, things were a little chaotic at Easy Nomad, a travel company. With the additional acquisition of two small overseas firms, the various branches were crowded with organizational policies and strategies whose interactions were producing results that no one wanted. Bubble diagrams were used to identify the areas of overlap between the policies. Managers were able to sort out the various inconsistencies, misalignments, and unintended consequences of the crowded policy and strategy areas.

The Strategic Change process has a single output – the creation of new criteria. The process produces revised or new criteria that are used to better align components with new strategic directions and allow a more accurate selection and review of components.

Question

Organizations need to be able to track new business conditions over time. Identify the examples of the tools that can be used to track and take into account strategic change.

Options:

1. Environmental consultants were brought in to assess whether global warming will affect the current Energy Usage portfolio

2. A change in client expectations caused portfolio management to re-weight three of the six criteria used for aligning the Customer Service portfolio

3. A multiple-criteria scoring model was used to evaluate components for inclusion in the Training portfolio

4. Bubble diagrams showing reduced consumer confidence were crucial in persuading portfolio management to revise the quality control criteria

5. A financial department's information system was linked to the central data repository to ensure easy reporting

Answer

Option 1: This is a correct option. Having consultants assess the potential long-term environmental impacts on strategy is an example of using expert judgment.

Option 2: This is a correct option. Re-weighted criteria for aligning components of a portfolio is a tool for incorporating strategic change.

Option 3: This is an incorrect option. The Strategic Change process tools are expert judgment, criteria re-weighting, and graphical representations, not particular scoring models.

Option 4: This is a correct option. A bubble diagram is just one of the graphical tools available for evaluating factors related to strategic change, and adjusting for them.

Option 5: This is an incorrect option. Reporting systems, such as central data repositories or financial data systems, are tools of the Portfolio Reporting and Review process not the Strategic Change process.

REFERENCES

References
- **A Guide to the Project Management Body of Knowledge (PMBOK® Guide), Fifth Edition** - 2009, Project Management Institute, Project Management Institute
- **The Complete Book of Project-Related Terms and Definitions: Mysteries Explained** - 2005, Mochal, Tom, TenStep, Inc.
- **Advanced Project Portfolio Management and the PMO: Multiplying ROI at Warp Speed** - 2003, Kendall, Gerald I. and Steven C. Rollins, J. Ross Publishing
- **Implementation: How to Transform Strategic Initiatives into Blockbuster Results** - 2006, Brache, Alan P. and Sam Bodley-Scott, McGraw-Hill
- **The Standard for Portfolio Management** - 2006, Ross, David W., PMP, et al, Project Management Institute

- **The Complete Project Management Handbook** - 2004, Hill, Gerard, Auerbach Publications
- **The AMA Handbook of Project Management, Second Edition** - 2006, Dinsmore, Paul C. and Jeannette Cabanis-Brewin

www.ingramcontent.com/pod-product-compliance
Lightning Source LLC
Chambersburg PA
CBHW020858180526
45163CB00007B/2546